Upgrading America:

The Political Writings
of
Zoltan Istvan

AUTHOR'S NOTE

While these essays have been arranged and edited for readability, some of them (if they are not new) appear similar to how they were originally published. Attempts have been made to preserve the context and moment in time they were written. Publishing information and fact checks can be found by utilizing the Appendix.

TABLE OF CONTENTS

CHAPTERS

III: Ideas that Challenge

****

CHAPTER I: UNCHARTED TERRITORY

1) The Growing World of Transhumanism

Transhumanists are curiosity addicts. If it's new, different, untouched, or even despised, we're probably interested in it. If it involves a revolution or a possible paradigm shift in human experience, you have our full attention. We are obsessed with the mysteries of existence, and we spend our time using the scientific method to explore anything we can find about the evolving universe and our tiny place in it.

Obsessive curiosity is a strange bedfellow. It stems from a profound sense of wanting something better in life—of not being satisfied. It makes one search, ponder, and strive for just about everything and anything that might improve existence. In the 21st century, that leads one right into transhumanism. That's where I've landed right now: A journalist, policy maker, and activist in the transhumanist movement. I advocate for science and tech-themed policies that give everyone the opportunity to live indefinitely in perfect health and freedom.

Politics aside, transhumanism is the international movement of using science and technology to radically change the human being and experience. Its primary goal is to deliver and embrace a utopian techno-optimistic world—a world that consists of biohackers, cyborgists, roboticists, life extension advocates, cryonicists, Singularitarians, and other science-devoted people.

Transhumanism was formally started in 1980's by philosophers in California. For decades it remained low key, mostly discussed in science fiction novels and unknown academic conferences. Lately, however, transhumanism seems to be surging in popularity. What once was a smallish band of fringe people discussing how science and technology can solve all humanity's problems has now become a burgeoning social mission of millions around the planet.

At the recent FreedomFest, the world's largest festival on liberty, transhumanism was a theme explored in numerous panels, including some I had the privilege of being on. Libertarian transhumanism is one of the fastest growing segments of American's freedom movement. A top priority for transhumanists is to have freedom from the government so radical science experiments and research can go on undisturbed and unregulated.

So why are so many people jumping on the transhumanist bandwagon? I think it has to do with the mishmash of tech inundating and dominating our daily lives. Everything from our smartphone addictions to flying at 30,000 feet in jet airplanes to Roombas freaking out our pets in our homes. Nothing is like it was for our forbearers. In fact, little is like it was even a generation ago. And the near future will be many times more dramatic: driverless cars, robotic hearts, virtual reality sex, and telepathy via mind-reading headsets. Each of these technologies is already here, and in some cases being marketed to billions of people. The world is shifting under our feet—and liberty-minded transhumanism is a sure way to navigate the chaos to make sure we arrive at the best future possible.

My interest in transhumanism began over 20 years ago when I was a philosophy and religion student at Columbia University in New York City. We were assigned to read an article on life extension techniques and the strange field of cryonics, where human beings are frozen after they've died in hopes of reviving them with better medicine in the future. While I'd read about these ideas in science fiction before, I didn't realize an entire cottage industry and movement existed in America that is dedicated to warding off death with radical science. It was an epiphany for me, and I knew after finishing that article I was passionately committed to transhumanism and wanted to help it.

However, it wasn't until I was in the Demilitarized Zone of Vietnam, on assignment for National Geographic Channel as a journalist, that I came to dedicate my life to transhumanism. Walking in the jungle, my guide tackled me, and I fell to the ground with my camera. A moment later he pointed at the half-hidden landmine I almost stepped on. I'd been through dozens of dangerous experiences in the over 100 countries I visited during my twenties and early thirties—hunting down wildlife poachers with WildAid, volcano boarding in the South Pacific, and even facing a pirate attack off Yemen on my small sailboat where I hid my girlfriend in the bilge and begged masked men with AK47s not to shoot me. But this experience in Vietnam was the one that forced a U-turn in my life. Looking at the unexploded landmine, I felt like a philosophical explosive had gone off in my head. It was time to directly dedicate my skills and hours to overcoming biological human death.

I returned home to America immediately and plunged into the field of transhumanism, reading everything I could on the topic, talking with people about it, and preparing a plan to contribute to the movement. I also began by writing my libertarian-minded novel *The Transhumanist Wager*, which went on to become a bestseller in philosophy on Amazon and helped launched my career as a futurist. Of course, a bestseller in philosophy on Amazon doesn't mean very many sales (there's been about 55,000 downloads to date), but it did mean that transhumanism was starting to appear alongside the ideas of Plato, Marx, Nietzsche, Ayn Rand, Sam Harris, and other philosophers that inspired people to look outside their scope of experience into the unknown.

And transhumanism is the unknown. Bionic arms, brain implants ectogenesis, artificial intelligence, exoskeleton suits, designer babies, gene editing tech. These technologies are no longer part of some Star Trek sequel, but are already here or being worked on. They will change the world and how we see ourselves as human beings. The conundrum facing society is whether we're ready for this. Transhumanists say yes. But America may not welcome that.

In fact, the civil rights battle of the century may be looming because of coming transhumanist tech. If conservatives think abortion rights are unethical, how will they feel about scientists who want to genetically combine the best aspects of species, including humans and animals together? And should people be able to marry their sexbots? Will transhumanist Christians try to convert artificial intelligence and lead us to something termed a Jesus Singularity? Should we allow scientists to reverse aging, something researchers have already had success with in mice? Finally, as we become more cyborg-like with artificial hips, cranial implants, and 3D-printed organs, should we rename the human species?

Whether people like it or not, transhumanism has arrived. Not only has it become a leading buzzword for a new generation pondering the significance of merging with machines, but transhumanist-themed columns are appearing in major media. Celebrity conspiracy theorists like Mark Dice and Alex Jones bash it regularly, and even mainstream media heavyweights like John Stossel, Joe Rogan, and Glenn Beck discuss it publicly. Then there's Google hiring famed inventor Ray Kurzweil as lead engineer to work on artificial intelligence, or J. Craig Venture's new San Diego-based genome sequencing start-up (co-founded with Peter Diamandis of the X-Prize Foundation and stem cell pioneer Robert Hariri) which already has 70 million dollars in financing.

It's not just companies either. Recently, the British Parliament approved a procedure to create babies with material from three different parents. Even President Obama, before he left office, jumped in the game by giving DARPA $70 million dollars to develop brain chip technology, part of America's multi-billion dollar BRAIN Initiative. The future is coming fast, people around the world are realizing, and there's no denying that the transhumanist age fascinates tens of millions of people as they wonder where the species might go and what health benefits it might mean for society.

At the end of the day, transhumanism is still really focused on one thing: satisfying that essential addiction to curiosity. With science, technology, and a liberty-minded outlook as our tools, the species can seek out and even challenge the very nature of its being and place in the universe. That might mean the end of human death by mid-century if governments allow the science and medicine to develop. It will likely mean the transformation of the species from biological entities into something with much more tech built directly into it. Perhaps most important of all, it will mean we will have the chance to grow and evolve with our families, friends, and loved ones for as long as we like, regardless how weird or wild transhumanist existence becomes.

****

2) We Must Transition from a Military-Industry Complex into A Science-Industrial Complex

Many Americans subscribe to the annoying belief that our nation's military-industrial complex is the surest way to remain the wealthiest and leading superpower in the world. After all, it's worked for the last century, pro-military supporters love to point out.

However, America's dependence on warmongering may soon become a liability that is impossible to maintain. Transhumanism, globalization, and outright replacement of human soldiers with robots are redefining the county's military requirements, and they may eventually render defense budgets far smaller than those now. To compensate and keep America spending approximately 20 percent of the federal budget on defense (as we have for most of the last few years), we'll either have to manufacture wars to use all our newly-made bombs, or find another way to keep the American economy afloat.

It just so happens that there is another way—a method that would satisfy liberals and conservatives alike. Instead of always spending more on our military, we could transition our nation and its economy into a scientific-industrial complex.

There's compelling reason to do this beyond what meets the eye. Transhumanist technology is starting to radically change human life. Many experts expect to be able to stop aging and conquer death for human beings in the next 25 years. Others, like myself, see humans merging with machines and replacing our every organ with bionic ones.

Such a new transhuman society will require many trillions of dollars to satisfy humans ever-growing desire for physical perfection (machine or biological) in the transhumanist age. We could keep our economy humming along for decades because of it.

Whatever happens, something is going to have to give in the future regarding military profiteering. Part of this is because in the past, the military-industrial complex operated off always keeping a few million US military members ready on a moment's notice to travel around the world and fight. But there's almost no scenario where we would need that kind of human-power (and infrastructure to support it) anymore.

Increasingly, small teams of special operation soldiers and uber-high tech are the way America fights its wars. We just don't need massive military bases anymore, nor the thousands of companies to support the constant maintenance of ground troops. Such a reality changes the economics of the military dramatically, and will eventually leave it a fraction of its size in terms of personnel and real estate.

We'll still have the need for technology to fight the wars and conflicts we entangle ourselves in, but it'll be mostly engineers, programmers, and technicians who wear the uniform. The coming military age of automated drones, robot tanks, cyberwarfare, and artificial intelligence just doesn't require that many people. In fact, expect the military not just to shrink, but to mostly disappear into ones and zeroes.

Many people think that the beast of a military-industrial complex—made famous by President Dwight Eisenhower's warning against it in his farewell address—appeared only in the last 50 years. However, others persuasively argue that America has been at war 93 percent of the time since the US Declaration of Independence was signed in 1776—so it's been with us from the beginning.

In liberal California where I live, such facts annoy just about everyone I know—except, of course, those who are shareholders and beneficiaries of the defense industry. Thankfully, despite Congress being led by mostly older white religious men, the younger generation clamors for an improved America—one that can keep its economies running smoothly in a more peaceful way.

This is where the scientific-industrial complex comes in and could satisfy most everyone. And best of all, a society of science requires actual people. Lots of them: nurses, scientists, start-up CEOs, designers, technologists, and even lawyers. The advent of modern medicine to treat virtually every ailment—and the whole anti-aging movement, in general—affects all 325+ million Americans. Over half of us suffer from health issues that can be improved but often aren't, for a variety of reasons. For example, the US Census Bureau reports that 40 percent of people over the age of 65 suffer from a disability—and for two thirds of them, it's mobility-related issues. And millions are already racking up the symptoms of heart disease that will kill them. And a younger generation is just waiting to explore bionics, chip implants, and how to upgrade their genes to avoid health problems in the future. All this means we have the fodder to reshape the American economy from a militaristic-based one to a type that thrives off scientific and medical innovation.

Instead of spending American money on sending our soldiers to risk their lives for the whims of war, we could be giving civilians the medicine and healthcare they need to live far better and longer. And living longer has unseen benefits, too. In the future, bonafide transhumans won't have to retire if they don't want to. Their bodies will be ageless and made so strong through technology that work and careers may continue indefinitely—and therefore, so will paying taxes. Transhuman existence is a self-fulfilling economic-boom prophesy for both individual and country.

To help create this new mindset in society, I recently delivered a *Transhumanist Bill of Rights* to the US Capitol as part of my presidential campaign tour. Article 1 of the bill, among other things, aims to establish that a nation would provide a universal right via science and technology for citizens to live indefinitely if they wanted. This, of course, takes universal healthcare (which I support via a Guaranteed Basic Income plan) one step further, and doesn't just mandate that the government is interested in your well-being, but that it's ultimately interested in your permanent survival.

If a nation was to embrace such a universal right to live indefinitely, it would forever change how a nation looks at the individual lives of its citizens. What would follow is a nation's intense build-out of how to improve the health, longevity, and well being of its people. Additionally, the institutions that are constantly drawing on America, like social security and welfare due to disability, would be less taxing.

Currently, the US Constitution (which I personally think needs a significant rewrite for the 21st century) is overly concerned with protection of national sovereignty—which is one major reason why the military-industrial complex is allowed to grow undeterred. If the US Constitution was endowed with precise wording to also protect an individual's health, well-being, and longevity, then a scientific-industrial complex could rise. This new monster institution would legally be mandated to provide the most modern medicine, technology, and science possible to its people.

Shamefully, the Iraq War will cost the US $6 trillion dollars by the time we're actually done paying all our bills—despite the fact that it's highly questionable whether Iraq was ever even a serious national security issue. However, our country undeniably faces a serious national security issue today—in fact, I'd call it a full blown crisis. Nearly 7,500 Americans will die in the next 24 hours from cancer, heart disease, diabetes, aging, and other issues. And the same amount of people will die tomorrow and the day after.

Overcoming disease and aging in the transhuman age will inevitably occur. The question is not if, but when? The answer lies in how much our nation is willing to spend on scientific and medical research—and how soon. But so long as it continues to spend money on the military instead of citizen's health, human beings will die—which is ironic since it's the military that is supposed to protect us (and not inadvertently sabotage us by swallowing funding for bombs instead of medicine). All we need do as a country is change the direction of our spending, from defense to science. If we can transform America into a scientific-industrial complex, we'll still be able to keep our economy chugging along. Let America's new wars be fought against cancer, diabetes, Alzheimer's, and aging itself. It's a win-win, except for body bag and casket makers

****

3) The Only Way to Fix the Earth's Environmental Issues is via New Technology

Earth Day came and went last week. And like years before, promises were made by governments and politicians to be better stewards of our planet. Just about any sane person realizes global warming is real and the damage humans have done to Planet Earth is substantial.

Most people believe a major step in the right direction to heal Earth's environmental crisis is to reduce humanity's carbon footprint and be more green—something being addressed in the recently signed Paris Agreement. While I applaud the collaborative effort and good intentions of the treaty, it's inadequate and doomed to failure. It's like bringing a water gun to a war zone. Nothing short of a mass-extinction event for humans can stop and reverse the environmental damage done or occurring to the planet. Billions of people around the developing world want the standard of life we have in America, and they're not going to stop for anything until they achieve that.

I don't know if the major US presidential candidates—are aware of this conundrum. And even if they were, the real question is: Can their politics, ethics, and religious beliefs handle it? Because sending out Christmas cards on recycled paper and giving tax incentives for electric cars is not going to pull us out of the toxic mess we've created on Earth. There's only one realistic hope to save the planet—and it comes from an unlikely place: technology. Radical technology. I'm talking CRISPR gene editing, transhumanism, geoengineering, and nanobots in every biological nook of the world. This will not be Kansas, anymore. And our current politicians will be freaked out by it.

The bright green future rests with disruptive tech. Consider this, for example: Twelve years ago, I used to work as a director at nonprofit wildlife organization WildiAid. In Cambodia, I went on undercover missions and helped bust and jail poachers who were causing wildlife—like tigers, Sun bears, and the Asian rhino—to go extinct. We did good work, but poaching is a nearly $20 billion business, and there's just no way a nonprofit organization (or even a dozen of them) could stop the demand for illegal wildlife, not when population growth in Asia is skyrocketing and poverty-stricken locals can sell a tiger for over $10,000.

But there are people who can save the endangered species on the planet. And they will soon dramatically change the nature of animal protection. Those people may have little to do with wildlife, but their genetics work holds the answer to stable animal population levels in the wild. In as little as five years, we may begin stocking endangered wildlife in places where poachers have hunted animals to extinction. We'll do this like we stock trout streams in America. Why spend resources in a losing battle to save endangered wildlife from being poached when you can spend the same amount to boost animal population levels ten-fold? Maye even 100-fold. This type of thinking is especially important in our oceans, which we've bloody well fished to near death.

As a US Presidential candidate who believes that all problems can be solved by science, I believe the best way to fix all of our environmental dilemmas is via technological innovation—not attempting to reverse our carbon footprint, recycle more, or go green.

As noted earlier, the obvious reason going green doesn't work—even though I still think it's a good disciplinary policy for humans—is the sheer impossibility of getting the developed world to stop... well, developing. You simply cannot tell an upcoming Chinese family not to drive cars. And you can't tell a burgeoning Indian city to only use renewable resources when it's cheaper to use fossil fuels. You also can't tell indigenous Brazilian parents to stop poaching when their children are hungry. These people will not listen. They want what they want, and are willing to partially destroy the planet to get it—especially when they know the developed world already possesses it.

So while I support green policies, there's no way such well-wishes will stop the future environmental degradation—nor will it reduce what already occurred. Even with a bunch of laws passed, or a massive cultural change, or everyone joining hands and singing "Kumbaya," we're in for dirty, toxic ride with the planet.

But don't lost hope. What can happen—and will likely happen barring a collapse of society—is our thriving modern world will devise transhumanist technological fixes to the issues at hand. Take meatless meat for example—a powerful disruptive idea already here. About a third of the arable land on earth is dedicated to grazing animals. Much of that land was slash-and-burned to make way for cattle and other livestock. If we switched to meatless meat, which is made in a laboratory and tastes quite similar to real meat, we could stop the clear cutting and whole scale destruction of those ecosystems (not to mention we can avoid cruelly slaughtering 150 million animals a day for food). Additionally, if we can figure out ways to genetically grow back rainforests in weeks instead of years, we could stop creating all that greenhouse crap that goes into our air and atmosphere. With new genetic editing techniques, it's quite possible we could learn to speed up biological processes, like tree and plant growth.

It gets even better, though. Gene-editing technology like CRISPR/Cas9 could in the future make us cancer-proof, so even if we did have a depleted ozone layer from rainforest destruction and pollution, we'd never get cancer. Another alternative is to use CRISPR tech to give us sunburn-proof skin.

Of course, plenty of prominent futurists are predicting a word of nanobots and nanotechnology in 20 years or less, which could physically change the structure of our material existence. We'd simply create billions of mini-robots that inhibit everything and help recreate and protect natural beauty. The nanobots and nanotech will be able to eradicate pollution and serve green purposes on a nearly molecular scale.

There's also geoengineering where we already have ways to do basic engineering on our climate. Rain is not something sent from the "gods," but the precise mixture of certain weather and atmospheric conditions, as China is already experimenting with. We are learning how to make it. We can be the new generation of rain makers—or of endless sunny days (though presumably we'd want a mixture of both). And we will soon be able to turn sand into forests, wastelands into nutrients for the planet, and uninhabitable land into pristine edens where humans thrive.

Whichever way you twist it, radical science is the method that can help and save us most efficiently. We can use it to fix just about every stupid thing we've ever done to our planet and to its life forms. And best of all, science often doesn't just tackle problems by kicking the proverbial can down the road, but rather by eradicating issues completely—like we did with diseases like smallpox, or by inventing freezers so our food doesn't spoil, or by flashlights so we can see outside on a rainy night.

But here is our impasse. Not every government leader is inclined to use science to fix the environment—or even to help human being's health and longevity. Some politicians believe first and foremost in following their moral and religious ideology—like former President George W. Bush, who severely limited federal stem cell funding for seven years while in office because of his Christian values.

With the radical new age of CRISPR genetic tech upon us, I'm worried that conservatives like Ted Cruz will also try to stop new technologies that will change our battle in combating a degrading Earth. It's likely Republicans will be against radical pro-green genetics or embracing environmentally-friendly cyborgism that seemingly counters their biblical view of the world. In this case, the Democrats—who are often far less religious than Republicans—may be more inclined to understand the necessity for changing our DNA or embracing nanotech to be become better climate-adjusters. In fact, maybe the Libertarians—who passionately insist on separation of church and state in public affairs—will be the most accepting of future tech to save the planet.

Like it or not, genetic editing, geoengineering, nanotech, and cyborgism are a fundamental part of the future for how we deal with basically everything, and it will allow us to rewrite the coding—and hence alter the form and purpose—of the entire biological world.

Sadly, there are already calls for moratoriums being voiced over some of these types of science. If there's a ban on the research, how then will we learn to re-grow trees in weeks instead of years to replenish our fragile rainforests? How will we help build up endangered wildlife populations if the technology is outlawed? How will we become cancer-proof to higher UV rays if we can't experiment?

Whatever happens in the US elections, if you care about the environment—if you care about really making a difference to return this planet back to a pristine and green state—then vote for the politician who doesn't make their science decisions based on archaic religion and 5,000-year-old holy texts, but on what works and what is in the best interest of the people. The next person in the White House is going to make or break the issue of environmentalism— and the greatest hope for them is to stand strong with using radical science and technology as their main weapon of change.

****

4) Technology Will Replace the Need for Big Government

The US Government has been expanding in size and reach for decades. The federal budget, deficit, and government employee base is near an all-time high.

It wasn't always like that. Many of America's founders were Libertarian-minded and skeptical of the state, wanting only those parts of the government that were absolutely necessary. However, there's reason to believe that in the near future, government might dramatically shrink—not because of demands by fiscally astute Americans, but because of radical technology.

Indubitably, millions of government jobs will soon be replaced by robots. Even the US President could one day be replaced, which—strangely enough—might bring sanity to our election process.

But it's not just robots, it's software programs and weird new tech that will do the replacing. Consider the over 1 million firefighters, a staple part of American government that also represents the ideal of service and career to one's country. Companies around the world are now building fireproof everything, including couches, furniture, and building materials that simply don't burn well. And intelligent robots—which I think will be in 50 percent of American households within five years time—will all have fire and carbon monoxide detectors.

In fact, I'm certain many in-home robots will not only be loaded with numerous security alert systems (like intruder alarms, flood warnings, and the ability to detect snakes, scorpions, and spiders) but will also be able to fix problems that occur. It's likely in just a few years time, in-home robots costing less than a $1,000 dollars will know how to put out a fire with an extinguisher, turn off a flooding bathtub, or squish a black widow.

Each time a robot or software can save an emergency call to a firefighter or police officer, money, time, and resources are saved. Twenty-five years into the future, we may have little reason to call any government service employee whatsoever—and institutions like the fire department may be significantly smaller.

The same idea goes for employees of the Internal Revenue Service, whose jobs crunching numbers can be done by even basic AI. Meanwhile, drones will replace building inspectors by flying around construction projects to determine safety and building requirements are being met. Even the tens of thousands of government highway workers will be replaced by driverless vehicles that automatically lay new roads down. Driverless construction equipment—just like a fully automated trucking industry—is the future. For that matter, even the White House may eventually turn to automated equipment such as driverless lawn mowers to cut its massive property lawns.

It's the military, though, where some of the robot revolution has already been witnessed on TV by many Americans. Instead of a company of troops on the ground, a single US soldier now sits in a military base on native soil controlling an armed drone thousands of miles away. America has approximately 2 million soldiers who can be quickly called up to service, but I think that number will quickly fall over the next decade as the US streamlines its military in the age of transhumanism—the age where machines do most of the work. Because national defense is such a large part of the Federal budget, this could save many billions of dollars for Americans.

Another area where technology can significantly help reduce government is the absurdly huge US prison system. Right now, it costs almost four times the amount of money to run America's nearly 5,000 prisons and jails than it does to run the US education system. But in the near future, we might use drones and robots to monitor criminals, both in and out of jail.

Many of our prisons are filled with nonviolent drug offenders, anyway, and I think we should let them all go free. If people and politicians are too afraid of that, we could just have drones or tracking devices monitor them. This way many nonviolent criminals could find jobs and start paying taxes—instead of being a drain on government resources. Another benefit would be that many prison guards wouldn't need to be employed either, as there would be less criminals to monitor. Perhaps best of all, emptied prisons and jails owned by the government could be used for other things, like new colleges or job training centers.

I welcome this future smaller government as a result of evolving technology, and I hope that Americans will pay less in taxes as a result of it. In fact, I think it's possible to offer more social services—including a Universal Basic Income—from the government to the people as a result of technology shrinking the administrative side. This would be a welcome arrangement, since the American government was founded to maximize the will and benefit of the people.

President John F. Kennedy famously said: "Ask not what your country can do for you—ask what you can do for your country." But he wasn't aware of the coming impact of the internet, the microprocessor, CRISPR gene editing technology, artificial intelligence, the robot revolution, or even people overcoming death with anti-aging science. He wasn't aware of how much this innovation would change the human race and the nature of government. If he had been, he might've said: "Ask not what your country can do for you—ask what technology your country should use to serve its citizens better."

****

5) Transhumanism is Under Siege from Socialism

Transhumanism—the burgeoning field of merging people with machines and synthetic components—is under siege by socialism. In the 1980s, when transhumanism first got started in California by libertarian-minded philosophers, few considered the political and economic ramifications of the movement. It was, after all, a movement heavily steeped in science fiction with little real-life technology to show. Today, with genetic engineering, artificial intelligence, and brain implants that can nearly connect us to the web, the movement is starting to affect every aspect of society. And those on the far left want to make sure the movement is advantageous for them.

Whether a social movement is embraced by the left or right can ultimately determine its course. Take environmentalism, for example, which has over a billion adherents. It's decidedly a movement associated with leftist political tendencies. In fact, many leaders in the GOP outright deny climate change despite notable scientific evidence, and our President has recently rolled back environmental regulations—all in a bid to push back against leftists gaining traction in this ever increasing hot-button political and social issue.

With its main goal of trying to stop biological death with science, transhumanism is growing quickly around the world—and could one day rival the environmental movement in scope and impact. Partially funded by Silicon Valley billionaires like Peter Thiel, Mark Zuckerberg, and Larry Ellison, transhumanism offers a view of the world that nothing is natural and everything is possible. But like all powerful social change, a challenging question remains: Who will be able to afford the technology?

While reputable formal studies don't exist, the transhumanism movement seems to be growing quickly in size, especially on Facebook and in social media. Over 100 internet groups exist, some with nearly 20,000 people each. Most of the recent growth in transhumanism seems to be coming from the youth. Over a third of Americans are under the age of 35, and a large majority that are voting age identify as independent or Democrats. It's for this reason, that transhumanism is turning left after years of being known as a libertarian-minded movement.

As a 46-year old transhumanist and former political candidate, I try to make my work and writings a bridge between the elder academics who started transhumanism and the youth where most of the growth of the movement appears to be. Despite my personal libertarian leanings, I try to incorporate all sides of the movement into one space to maintain cohesion. I'm not sure it's working well, as I'm increasingly seeing a more pronounced tug-of-war to define transhumanism's direction and social values to veer hard left.

Take bioethicist Alex Pearlman's recent story on the front page of *Medium*. It was titled: *The Misguided Idiot's Quest for Immortality: A diatribe on the folly and privilege of the Transhumanist movement.* Like the title suggests, it assumes transhumanism is for the rich, and is therefore basically anti-society. Pearlman doubles down on the biggest question left-leaning transhumanists ask: How will we keep the rich from hoarding all the best technology for themselves and leaving the rest of society behind?

It's a valid question, though it smells of 20th Century robber baron talk. In the 21st Century, tech billionaires are sometimes known as much for their money as their humanitarian deeds. The Bill and Melinda Gates Foundation is an example. So is Mark Zuckerberg and his wife's multi-billion dollar donation to eradicate all disease by the end of the century.

Ultimately, I believe the so-called One Percent—the very richest of society—don't desire to leave the rest of the world behind by taking radical transhumanist upgrades only for themselves. I think many young superrich are partially humbled by their successes and want to spend vast amounts of their wealth to make the world better. Many successful tech entrepreneurs I know—most who are fun-loving geeks at heart—are ultimately altruistic, and not personalities that obsessively want to always outdo their neighbors. Many seem almost guilty of their newfound wealth, and some of them make a point of sharing it through visionary nonprofit programs in order to give something back to the world.

Despite this, one look at liberal media, and it's easy to see that transhumanism and its wealthy patrons are getting a bad rap. Journalists—many who are science lovers themselves—often accuse technology leaders of steering humanity into a dystopian future. Reading much of the negativity about transhumanism that now comes out frequently, it's easy to see that many of the article's journalists support increased big government and even believe capitalism might be outright philosophically wrong.

The real threat of transhumanism succumbing to socialism is not that it turns left, but that competition and free markets is rooted from the creation and distribution of its technology. We need healthy competition in any endeavor humanity pursues—something the 20th Century geo-political climate and the fall of the Soviet Union taught us all too well. In the near future, though genetic engineering, neural augmentation, and bionic organs and body parts, we may not all be born equal—or even be the same fundamental species. However, to remain on equal footing in the world, we must stand behind the advancing field of transhumanism with its historical impulses of liberty as a topmost concern. Socialism has a long, violent history of precisely not doing that—of strangling emerging social movements—so transhumanists must be on their guard against it. Transhumanists must favor the free world and free market to make its movement as powerful and successful as possible.

****

6) Genetic Editing Could Cause the Next Cold War

While *Time* magazine recently chose President-Elect Donald Trump as its Person of the Year, CRISPR gene editing pioneers were a runner-up choice. Few innovations in the last millennium carry such transformative prospects as the ability to edit our own genome and make ourselves into fundamentally something else. Some experts think genetic editing might be the key to curing all disease and achieving perfect health.

Unlike other epic scientific advances—like the 1945 explosion of the first atomic bomb in New Mexico—the immediate effect of genetic editing technology is not dangerous. Yet, it stands to be just as divisive to humans as the 70-year proliferation of nuclear weaponry. On one hand, you have secular-minded China and its scientists leading the gene editing revolution, openly modifying the human genome in hopes of improving the human being. On the other hand, you have a Republican US administration that appears to be strongly Christian—conservatives who often insist humans should remain just as God created them.

Therein lies a great coming conflict, one that I'm sure will lead to street protests, riots, and civil strife—the kind described explicitly in my novel *The Transhumanist Wager*, where a religious-fundamentalist government shuts down extreme science in the name of conservatism. The playing field of geopolitics is pretty simple: If China or another country vows to increase its children's intelligence via genetic editing (which I estimate they will be able to do in 6-12 years' time), and America chooses to remain "au naturel" because they insist that's how God made them, a conflict species-deep will quickly arise. If this scenario seems too bizarre to happen, just consider the Russian Olympic track and field team that was banned in the recent 2016 Games for supposed doping.

It's quite possible the same accusatory flavor of "banning" could happen between China and America in the game of life—between its workers, its politicians, is people, its artists, and its media. I wonder if America—approximately 70 percent who identify as Christians—will put up with beings who modified themselves by science to be smarter and more functional entities.

This type of idea takes racism and immigration to a whole new level. Will America close off its borders, its jobs, its schools, and its general openness to the world to stay pure, old-fashioned human? Will we stop trading, befriending, and even starting families with those who are modified?

In short, will genetic editing start a new cold war? One that bears much finger pointing and verbal reprimands, including the use of derogatory terms like mutants, cyborgs, and transhumanists. Think the videogame Dues Ex, but with modified people taking all the best jobs. In a worst-case scenario, it could even start a World War.

So, now that we know what can happen if America won't embrace the most important science to emerge this century, how can we avoid it?

First—and this is wishful thinking, since 100 percent of the US Congress and the Supreme Court appear to be religious at the moment—is we could just embrace genetic editing and be better at it than the Chinese. This is the exact scenario I suggest. Yes, it will lead to a place where beings are similar to those in Star Wars and Star Trek, but after all, we love those stories because we want to reach that super-science age. And in the long run, such evolution of the species is inevitable anyway, so long as we don't kill ourselves first in a nuclear war or an environmental catastrophe.

In a second scenario, America could focus more on technology and less on biology and genetics. On my recent 4-month long Immortality Bus tour across America, I found conservative people seem more inclined to use tech accessories or wear a special headset that would make them smarter (for example, by connecting their thoughts Matrix-style into the cloud and AI)—as opposed to structurally changing their brains, as the Chinese likely will do. America could innovate that accessory tech that would keep us ahead of the biological modifications of other nations. I'll accept that—reluctantly—if the first scenario I presented is a no-go.

A third way—and this is the blatant transhumanist nightmare—is we could establish a non-modification policy across all countries, similar to how we have created the Paris Treaty for climate change or rules of war that ban chemical weapons. The major nations of the world, sensing a significant global legal issue in genetic editing, could come together as a species and criminalize the science.

To some extent, this has already happened, because as soon as the world realized the Chinese had experimented on the human genome, calls were made to put a stop on some of this science. Such a reaction is not dissimilar from what George W. Bush did with stem cells when his religious values made him shut down federal funding on all but a tiny portion of the research in America. Stem cells have since been shown to be one of the most important medical applications in the world, and those lost years of science have potentially negatively affected millions of lives.

Sadly, the third option of a general or even partial moratorium on genetic editing will surely harm innovation. The great thing with gene editing is we can likely do many wondrous things with it, such as potentially cure cancer, halt aging, grow better organs, and overcome disability by better repairing ourselves. Beyond making ourselves superhuman, we can simply make ourselves better fit for Earth, including dealing with a changing environment.

I also don't think the third option will work in the long run. More than ever, science is the hands of individuals, who can buy amazing bio-testing kits on eBay for just a $1000—as well as incredibly powerful computers to analyze the data. Citizen scientists would just create the new gene editing tech and begin doing it themselves—perhaps more dangerously had the government not been overseeing the research from the start.

I argue for the first path. Let's allow good, old-fashioned scientific competition with China to proceed. Let's see which country can create the best enhancements for their citizenry, and let's share the best of our work with one another in the end to make it so all peoples are as equal as possible. If we're too closed-minded about such radical science, we might find ourselves embroiled in a state of hostile speciation, where another new cold war—or worse— swallows a generation.

****

7) An AI Global Arms Race is Looming

Forget about superintelligent AIs being created by a company, university, or a rogue programmer with Einstein-like IQ. Hollywood and its AI-themed movies like *Transcendence* and *Her* have misled the public. The launch of the first truly autonomous, self-aware artificial intelligence—one that has the potential to become far smarter than human beings—is a matter of the highest national and global security. Its creation could change the landscape of international politics in a matter of weeks—maybe even days, depending on how fast the intelligence learns to upgrade itself, hack and rewrite the world's best codes, and utilize weaponry.

In the last few years, a chorus of leading technology experts, like Elon Musk, Stephen Hawking, and Bill Gates, have chimed in on the dangers regarding the creation of AI. The idea of a superintelligence on Planet Earth dwarfing the capacity of our own brains is daunting. Will this creation like its creators? Will it embrace human morals? Will it become religious? Will it be peaceful or warlike? The questions are innumerable and the answers are all debatable, but one thing is for sure from a national security perspective: If it's smarter than us, we want it to be on our side—the human race's side.

Now take that one step further, and I'm certain another theme regarding AI is just about to emerge—one bound with nationalistic fervor and patriotism. Politicians and military commanders around the world will want this superintelligent machine-mind for their countries and defensive forces. And they'll want it exclusively. Using AI's potential power and might for national security strategy is more than obvious—it's essential to retain leadership in the future world. Inevitably, a worldwide AI arms race is set to begin.

As a policy maker, I don't mind going out on a limb and saying the obvious: I also want AI to belong exclusively to America. Of course, I would hope to share the nonmilitary benefits and wisdom of a superintelligence with the world, as America has done for much of the last century with its groundbreaking innovation and technology. But can you imagine for a moment if AI was developed and launched in, let's say, North Korea, or Iran, or increasingly authoritarian Russia? What if another national power told that superintelligence to break all the secret codes and classified material that America's CIA and NSA use for national security? What if this superintelligence was told to hack into the mainframe computers tied to nuclear warheads, drones, and other dangerous weaponry? What if that superintelligence was told to override all traffic lights, power grids, and water treatment plants in Europe? Or Asia? Or everywhere in the world except for its own country? The possible danger is overwhelming.

Below is something simple I've designed that's tautological in nature called the "AI Imperative." It demonstrates why an AI arms race is likely in humanity's future:

1) According to experts, a superintelligent AI is likely possible to create, and with enough resources, could be developed in a short amount of time (such as in 10-20 years).

2) Assuming we can control this superintelligent AI, whoever launches it first will likely always have the strongest superintelligence indefinitely, since that AI can be programmed to undermine and control all other AIs—if it allows any others to develop at all. Being first is everything in the superintelligent AI creation game (imagine if you were first to develop the Atomic bomb, and then also had the power to limit who else could ever develop one).

3) Whichever government launches and controls a superintelligent AI first will almost certainly end up the most powerful nation in the world because of it.

Given the AI Imperative, there's really only two likely courses of action for the world, even though there's four major possibilities on how to proceed. The first is to make AI development illegal all around the world—similar to chemical weapon development.

However, people and companies probably would not go for it. We are a capitalistic civilization and the humanitarian benefits of AI are too promising to not create it. Stopping development of technology has never really worked, either. Someone else just ends up eventually doing it—either openly or in secret—if there's gain or profit to be made.

The other option is to be the first to create the superintelligent AI. That's the one my money is on—the one America is going to pick, regardless which political party is in office. America's military will likely spend as much of its resources as it needs to make sure it has exclusivity or majority control in the launch of a superintelligent AI. I'm guessing that trillions of dollars will be spent on AI development by the American military over the next ten years, regardless of national debt, economic conditions, or public disagreement. I'm betting that engineers, coders, and even hackers will become the new face of the American military, too. Our new warriors will be geeks working around the clock in the highest security environment possible. Think the Manhattan Project, but many more times in size and complexity.

Of course a third option is that AI is developed via a broad international consortium. However, nuclear weapon proliferation shows why, at least so far, this idea will likely not come to pass—at least on a worldwide level. As long as powerful nations like Russia and China independently push their flavor of social policy, economic development, and government operations (many of which largely mirror their leader's desires), this is unlikely to work or be accepted. This is because we're not talking about good old fashioned teamwork exploring outer space together on the space station or stopping developing-world civil wars and genocides, as the respected United Nations sometimes is involved in. We're talking about military power and protection of our families, citizenry, and livelihoods. There's much less room for cooperation when it concerns such personal matters.

A fourth option, one that I believe may be inevitable in the long run, is that all nations unite democratically and politically under one flag, one elected leadership, and one government, in an effort to better control the technology that is ushering in the transhumanist age— such as superintelligent AI. Then, all together, we create this intelligence. I like the sound of this from a philosophical and humanitarian point of view. The problem with it is such a plan takes time and many proud people to swallow their egos and cultural differences—and with only about 10 to 20 years before superintellitent AI is created, no one is going to push hard for that option.

So, inevitably, we are back to our looming dog-eat-dog AI arms race. It may not be one filled with nuclear fallout shelters like yesteryear, but it will show all the signs of the most powerful nations and the best minds they posses vying against one another for an all-important future national security. More importantly, it's a winner-takes-all scenario. The competition of the century is set to begin.

****

8) Secular Advocate: Religion is Harming Society and Lives

All around the world, religious terror is striking and threatening us. Whether in France, Turkey, London, or the USA, the threat is now constant. We can fight it all we want. We can send out our troops; we can chip refugees; we can try to monitor terrorist's every move. We can even improve trauma medicine to deal with extreme violence they bring us. But none of this solves the underlying issue: Abrahamic religions like Christianity and Islam are fundamentally violent philosophies with violent Gods. Sam Harris, Richard Dawkins, Christopher Hitchens and others have all reiterated essentially the same thing.

Consider these verses from the Koran:

Koran (3:56): As to those who reject faith, I will punish them with terrible agony in this world and in the Hereafter, nor will they have anyone to help.

Koran (8:12): I will cast terror into the hearts of those who disbelieve. Therefore strike off their heads and strike off every fingertip of them.

And then consider these verses from the Bible:

Deuteronomy 17:12: Anyone arrogant enough to reject the verdict of the holy man who represents God must be put to death. Such evil must be purged.

Numbers: 31:17: Now therefore kill every male among the little ones, and kill every woman that hath known man by lying with him.

Of course, both the Koran and Bible have passages that highlight kindness too—but you don't get a get-out-of-jail-free card in the 21st Century by being both violent and peaceful. If you beat your spouse, you're an abuser and can face jail time (even if you're a loving spouse other times). It's one or the other in the 21st Century: If you're a warmonger, murderer, or a terrorist—you're a bona fide warmonger, murder, or terrorist. And nothing is going to change that.

The fundamental problem with religion is that believers—about 5 billion people right now on Planet Earth—are so sure they're "correct" on anything and everything they believe. This is, of course, a sure sign of insanity—especially since most of what people believe was taught to them when they were children (and they had no way to filter it out or reason about it).

The only real truth out there, at least while our brains are just three pound bags of meat (and our senses—like our eyes—see just 1 percent of the visible universe), is to know "absolute truth" is something way too complex to understand. The only real thing to understand right now is the Scientific Method—the holy grail of wisdom that reason advocates follow. It states that if you test a hypothesis enough times, and the outcome seems to always be similar, then you can utilize that as a semi-truth and apply it functionally in one's life (but beware: It could change anytime and it might). That's the language of reason—the language of science.

It's the same method of thinking that explains why jet airplanes don't fall out of the sky. Or why skyscrapers keep standing through hurricanes. Or why we could put a man on the moon and bring him back.

However, it's not the thinking method that President Obama used to swear on a Bible to get his job on inauguration day. Or George W. Bush when he stopped life saving stem cell funding for seven years during his presidency. Or the Pope when he insists condom usage is a sin, despite it having the possibility of saving millions of lives from AIDS in Africa.

The Scientific Method is also not the thinking method of the pilots who flew into the World Trade Center. Or of the murderer who gunned down people in Orlando. And it's certainly not the method of thinking that the truck driver used to run down innocent people in Nice, France.

Like the hundreds of millions of other nonreligious people out there, it's hard for me to fathom how religious people got brainwashed into being this way—this ignorant. But bear in mind, it's not just religious terrorism that is literally killing us—it's much more.

Consider how many nonreligious secular people there are leading our nation right now. The answer is astonishing: It's zero (at least publicly). All 535 members of Congress, all nine Supreme Court justices, and our President believe in God and an afterlife.

No wonder life extension and anti-aging science is basically unfunded by the US Government. Why should the US care about whether you live longer or can overcome disease when you're all going to wake up in Jesus' arms after you die? Or in some heavenly Islamic paradise with a bunch of virgins?

I'm a political candidate that wants you to live—not in some unknown paradise once you die that no one has ever seen before or can prove exists. I want you to live now, regardless what craziness or tragedy the world can throw at you. I want your loved ones to live too—and not die because of aging, disease, or terrorism. I want you all to survive as long as you want—and to try to find a perfect world here on Earth. Transhumanist science can give that to us, and it will soon. And maybe in a hundred years, we can all even venture somewhere else in the universe when space travel can get us there safely.

If you want to live—and not be killed or die—make a point to criticize and disavow religion and religious people for being deathist: the idea that death is either welcome or acceptable (whether it comes via terrorism, disease, or aging).

In the 21st Century, fundamental religion is a form of mental disease. And sadly, that disease continues to take lives everywhere, in the worst of ways.

****

9) The New American Dream: Let the Robots Take our Jobs

Many of us wake in the mornings to a dreaded alarm clock. After breakfast, we jump into our cars, battle traffic, and start a tiring 9 to 5 at work. Then we come home, turn on the tube, sip a beverage, and mostly veg. We do that all week long, waiting for the weekend when we might actually get time to travel somewhere, enjoy a hobby, or complete a fun project. Then we repeat, and it's only broken up by our measly two-week vacation. The American Dream is not so much a pilgrimage anymore, but a well-greased hamster wheel. We have been cajoled into an economic system that needs to infinitely grow in order to feed itself and feel satiated.

In the transhumanist age we are now entering, the same philosophy of keeping up with the Joneses is increasingly becoming a less viable economic policy. And the robots and software applications the Joneses are building to take our jobs are simply not something we can or should attempt to compete against. We won't win.

However, as human beings, we can evolve and be happier and more fulfilled than we've ever been before. The key is a shift in our thinking—and in the value we place in the kind of work we want to do and how we enjoy free time.

The near-term socioeconomic forecasts are pretty startling when you look closely at them. *The Washington Post* recently ran an essay pointing out that 3.5 million truck drivers are poised to lose their jobs when the trucking industry becomes driverless (which could start happening in about two years, I believe). The trucking industry is just one of hundreds of sectors that could become significantly automated within a decade.

For example, *Business Insider* recently shared footage of a robot doing the work of a food server in China—the restaurant owner bought the robot for a mere $13,000. Home improvement giant Lowes already has robots on some of its floors. Some hotel check-ins are now automated too, eliminating the need for receptionists. Few if any jobs, including those of journalists, lawyers, doctors, and politicians, are totally protected from automation anymore.

Like many other people, you're probably asking yourself: How can this possibly be a good thing? The simple answer is: It will be a good thing only if we make it one. To begin with, there's no point in pretending society can avoid a future Universal Basic Income (UBI)—one that meets basic living standards—of some sort in America and around the world if robots or software take most of the jobs. I prefer leasing out America's $200 trillion dollars worth of federal land and natural resources (called a Federal Land Dividend) to provide a basic income. But other ideas—largely progressive or liberal ones—include income redistribution via taxes, increased welfare, or a mass guaranteed basic income plan tech and robot companies exclusively pay. Either way, without some type of basic income in the future, there will be mass revolutions that could end in a dystopian civilization—leading essentially to what experts call a societal collapse.

Those are the basic options, since history and common sense tells us it's impossible to maintain a peaceful, free society with the rich growing wealthier due to cheaper labor and the rest of society growing poorer due to lack of income. Since I do believe that democracy generally works, I think people will eventually vote for the best interest of the majority—which will soon be comprised of the jobless on our current trajectory. I also tend to believe the rich of the world will want to see democracy thrive, something that has helped all classes and types of people prosper. The elite may not want to part with some of their money (I myself support many libertarian ideas) via wealth redistribution, but I think they probably want to avoid an ugly dystopian world even more—especially one where they would be despised rulers.

Of course, there are other, more radical alternatives, too. Susanne Tarkowski Tempelhof, Founder & CEO of Bitnation says, "To the contrary of what many people think, Basic Income doesn't have to be a socialist-leaning concept, it can be done on an entirely voluntary basis, through using the Bitcoin Blockchain technology, charging a fee on top of transactions, if people accept to pay that fee. Here at Bitnation we believe that as the world becomes more transhumanist, the nation state will loose relevance naturally—so avoiding national tax collection schemes in favor of voluntary contribution to online platforms is a more long term sustainable approach."

Whatever the future brings, it should also not be overlooked that the main goals when humanity creates technology is to gain freedom and prosperity. Broadly speaking, that is exactly what has occurred so far in history. Experts point out that technology is widely responsible for the positive progress the world has experienced since the Industrial Revolution. In the last few decades, that progress is even more pronounced. More people on planet Earth—regardless of wealth—are healthier, more educated, and living longer, according to a recent report from The World Bank. Just about every aspect of human experience has improved across the world as a result of technology. This will likely continue as further tech innovation occurs, even when—especially when—robots take our jobs.

As a political candidate, I am hoping to further this improved standard of living that is being experienced everywhere. I specifically advocate for some free education at all levels (including higher education) paid for by my Federal Land Dividend. In fact, I support increased education levels, too, including some forms of mandatory preschool and 4-year college for everyone.

After all, if people are living twice as long as before (most people born today will live at least 125 years, many experts say), education should also be lengthened. The thing with education is it gives people time to think about what they really want to do in life. And I don't mean how to better keep up with the Joneses and their robots—I mean discovering their own inner passion and skills. Maybe it's art. Maybe it's engineering. Maybe it's sports. Maybe it's science. Whatever it is, a longer, more in depth education gives a person's spirit and mind the proper environment to decide what its heart is all about.

In the future—with less work and responsibility due to robots taking our jobs and leaving us only to collect our UBI—we might find there is a lot more to life than buying the latest trinkets from Walmart, or zoning out late at night in front of a television, or worrying about how poorly our bosses treat us at work. I say let the robots come. They may take our jobs, but they bring us freedom as well. With that freedom, we can become the best human beings we are capable of—a people full of passion, education, and a newly discovered drive of what it means to be alive. Perhaps it's time to reimagine the American Dream.

****

CHAPTER II: DISCOVERING POLICIES

10) The Abortion Debate is Stuck. Artificial Wombs are the Answer

Could an emerging technology reshape the battle lines in the abortion debate? Since Roe v. Wade was decided in 1973, that fight has been defined by the interlocking, absolute values of choice and life: For some, a woman's right to choose trumps any claim to a right to life by the fetus; for others, it's the reverse. But what if we could separate those two — what if a woman's choice to terminate a pregnancy no longer meant terminating the fetus itself?

That is the promise of artificial wombs, a technology that has already shown some success in tests on sheep fetuses. Early in a ewe's pregnancy, the lamb fetus is removed from her body and placed in a synthetic uterine environment in which it receives nutrients and fluids, and continues to develop to term, a process researchers call ectogenesis.

Artificial human wombs are still far in the future, and there are of course other ethical issues to consider. But for now, the technology is developed enough to raise new questions for the abortion debate.

In a 2017 issue of the journal Bioethics, two philosophers, Jeremy V. Davis, a visiting professor at the United States Military Academy at West Point, and Eric Mathison, a postdoctoral associate at Baylor College of Medicine, argue that while a woman has a right to remove a fetus from her body, she does not have the right to kill it. The problem is that, for now, the latter is inherent in the former.

Their argument builds upon that of the pro-choice philosopher Judith Jarvis Thompson, who famously argued in her 1971 paper "A Defense of Abortion" that women have a right to not carry a fetus for nine months — but that women do not have a right to be guaranteed the death of the fetus.

Such arguments point toward a disjunction in the abortion debate. Ectogenesis is the answer.

Synthetic wombs have an appeal far beyond the abortion debate, of course. They could revolutionize premature birth, which the World Health Organization calls the number one cause of death among children under 5.

The most advanced research in ectogenesis is underway at Children's Hospital of Philadelphia, where sheep fetuses have been removed from their mothers' bodies after 105 to 120 days — the equivalent, in a human, of 22 to 24 weeks — and placed in "biobags," clear plastic containers filled with amniotic fluid. So far the lambs have developed with few complications.

Biobag technology could be available for humans in as little as one to three years, according to Dr. Alan Flake, a fetal surgeon in charge of the Children's Hospital of Philadelphia artificial womb experiments. Another team performing ectogenesis research at the University of Michigan also believes they could have devices ready for humans in a similar time frame.

Some major supporters of artificial wombs are transhumanists, who believe in using technology to improve human health, intelligence and quality of life. Women's rights activists likewise support the research, aiming to free the female body.

But the promise of artificial wombs should appeal most to conservatives looking to reduce the 600,000 abortions performed annually in the United States (50 million abortions worldwide annually), but pessimistic about the chance of overturning Roe any time soon. Every fetus that was going to be aborted but instead makes it into an artificial womb could be considered a life saved.

Dr. Daniel Deen, an assistant professor of philosophy at Concordia University in Irvine, Calif., recently said in an interview with the website *Leapsmag*: "If the technology gets developed, I could not see any Christians, liberal or conservative, arguing that people seeking abortion ought not opt for a 'transfer' versus an abortive procedure."

Obviously, the idea that science could short-circuit a moral debate is discomforting for some. As artificial wombs improve, biobags are likely to become a hot-button topic for conservatives, who will have to decide how far they want to use technology to accomplish their ethical goals.

There are practical challenges, too: Artificial womb transplants and births are sure to be dramatically more expensive than the typical 15-minute abortion procedure, which costs around $500. And if even a quarter of those fetuses that would have been aborted are brought to term artificially, 150,000 babies a year would be born, almost all of them likely to be put up for adoption — more than the total number of annual adoptions in the United States. Who will pay for those procedures, and who will care for those children once they are born?

It is unlikely that the abortion debate will be resolved soon — certainly not as a legal matter. But as a practical and philosophical one, artificial wombs offer a way for both sides in the debate to move forward. The only question is whether we are willing to accept the increasingly central — and beneficial — role that technology can play in resolving what were once considered immutable human problems.

****

11) In the Transhumanist Age We Should be Fixing Disabilities not Sidewalks

Major media is reporting on what is being billed as a landmark agreement for the physically disabled community. A court has ordered the city of Los Angeles to spend $1.3 billion dollars over the next three decades to fix its dilapidated network of sidewalks and access ways, many of which are in disrepair and present challenges for people with disabilities to traverse.

Such a massive amount of money sets a precedent for other similar lawsuits to take place in America. If we take the largest 50 cities in the US, and just half of them agree to similar actions over the next decade, there might be another $25 billion dollars going to giving people with disabilities better sidewalks.

On the surface, this seems like great news for those who have mobility issues. However, with so much radical transhumanist technology being invented in the 21st Century—like exoskeleton suits—should society instead try to use that money to eliminate physical disability altogether?

America has long history with what can be called bandage culture—the idea that quick fixes are acceptable, even if they don't eliminate the root of the problem. Take heart disease for example, the #1 killer in America. We spend approximately $500 billion every year treating cardiovascular disease. However, with a market cap of only about $300 million dollars, French company Carmat could change the entire field with its new robotic heart. Carmat recently successfully installed a permanent artificial heart in a patient. If all goes well, in 10 years' time, humans may have the option to electively replace our biological hearts for better robotic hearts—thereby possibly wiping out heart disease.

The question is: Why hasn't America, its government, and its numerous multi-billion dollar healthcare and biotech companies actually ended heart disease, instead of just treating it? Clearly, we haven't been tackling these issues in the best way possible, as Carmat is doing.

In the case of people with disabilities getting better sidewalks, I'm wondering if the nearly three million Americans in wheel chairs might rather have exoskeleton suits that allow them to run, jump, and play active sports. Exoskeleton technology is poised to become one of the most important innovations of the decade, affecting not only people with disabilities, but also the obese and the elderly—which together account for nearly a third of the American population.

But exoskeleton tech is still an industry in its infancy. It's safe to say that if America invested $25 billion dollars into the industry, it would significantly speed up the development of advanced exoskeleton suits and bionic apparatuses. Then, instead of people with disabilities navigating crumbling sidewalks on their wheelchairs, they might soon be running over them at 15 miles per hour while jogging.

Additionally, it's not just exoskeleton tech that can help people with disabilities. There's also the possibility of combining exoskeleton tech with wheelchair innovation. Engineer and neuroscientist John

Hewitt, who frequently writes on technology, emailed me, "Even wheelchairs that shape-shift a bit to get people up to eye level once in a while would have a great benefit on the disabled."

Hewitt also thinks intrusive exoskeleton tech could be useful. He writes, "They are devices that draw on some intact sensory or motor capabilities still working in the user. It's a peripheral that now skirts the definition of a true bionic system, and it integrates at some level either at that of the peripheral nerve, subsurface brain, and/or osseointegration with the musculoskeletal system."

Another method would be to just outright cure various physical disabilities. The field of stem cell technology, where damaged body areas—such as the spine—can be potentially rejuvenated with healthy cells, is showing much promise.

Whatever direction the technology evolves towards, there are plenty of useful ways to spend resources to significantly improve the mobility of those with physical disabilities. Unfortunately, a closer look at the Los Angeles lawsuit reveals that some of the people benefiting most are, not surprisingly, lawyers, who are making off with millions of dollars after the court case. To be fair, however, fixing sidewalks will provide many people construction jobs. And cement and wheelchair makers are probably happy with the billion dollar settlement too.

But if you really want to consider the macro economic picture, imagine if we could give the physically disabled the real ability to be mobile again. Many Americans' disabilities prove too much for them to be currently employed, but exoskeleton and other types of technology would give them the means to jump right back into the work force. With millions of people in the US suffering from mobility issues, it would be far more lucrative for the country to have its people with disabilities employed, rather than giving them level sidewalks.

Ultimately, America's bandage culture is symptomatic of an economic and political system that is based on being too "politically correct." Too often, our nation talks about helping the poor, or the disenfranchised, or the underrepresented by doing good deeds and passing laws to protect those people. Sadly, what often happens is society ends up entombing this group in further despair and neglect, instead of offering it real means to eliminate its problems.

As a political candidate, I advocate for doing whatever is necessary to eliminate physical disability altogether. We are shortchanging our citizens and our country by not doing otherwise. In the 21st Century, with so much technology and radical medicine at our fingertips, we should reconsider the Americans with Disability Act. It's great to have a law that protects against discrimination, but in the transhumanist age we also need a law that insists on eliminating disability via technology and modern medicine.

In Los Angeles, I suggest spending 20 percent of the $1.3 billion dollar award for the very worst sidewalks—and then having the rest go directly into research and development for technologies that over a 10-year period of time will help eliminate physical disability. If all American cities agreed to this approach, potentially $20 billion dollars could be amassed. A national investment entity with public oversight could then spread that money to the most talented engineers, scientists, universities, and companies in the country— most whose current research budgets for overcoming physical disability are only in the tens of millions of dollars, at best. With $20 billion dollars of funding to spread around, we could forever change the hardship of physical disability in America and worldwide.

In short, let the sidewalks remain in disrepair. Instead, in the transhumanist age we're now in, let's work to repair physically disabled human beings, and make them mobile and able-bodied again.

****

12) I Advocate for the Legalization of All Drugs

I'm from San Francisco. Doing drugs—especially smoking pot— seems second nature to me. I've made a point of trying nearly all drugs, and I'm unabashedly proud of that fact. I consider Aldous Huxley's *The Doors of Perception* one of the most important books I read in my youth, and I've often wondered if it should be mandatory that everyone try a hallucinogenic drug at least once in their lives.

Almost all transhumanists welcome and endorse mind-altering substances. We thrive off change, experimentation, and new experiences, including wild drug trips with friends. For transhumanists, trying drugs is not just about having fun, but about self-amelioration and becoming the best, most enlightened versions of ourselves.

I'm campaigning across the country, sometimes talking about a Transhumanist Bill of Rights I delivered to the US Capitol. One of those rights include language that advocates for citizens being able to take any drugs they want, so long as the taking of it doesn't directly hurt someone else.

Unfortunately, while California—which is home to many transhumanist-minded organizations and companies, like Google and Apple—breeds a culture of open-mindedness, many states in the South don't.

Perhaps no state demonstrates this better than Arkansas, which ironically bills itself as "The Natural State." While many states at least allow marijuana to be administered medically to terminally ill patients, Arkansas does no such thing. Pot is totally illegal.

My bus and presidential campaign drove into Little Rock, Arkansas to meet with Rick Morgan, a proponent of the cannabis legalization effort in the state.

"It's incredible to me that if a dying person wants to smoke a little weed to help with their last days, it's not allowed," Morgan told me.

Morgan runs a number of stores that sell cannabis related items, and is also the creator of Realbud Camo, which makes camouflaged shirts using marijuana plant images.

Morgan told me when someone refuses to give marijuana to a dying person that wants it, he considers that appalling.

I agree with him. In fact, I believe it should be crime to not allow mild recreational drugs to people who want them.

"There are nearly three million people who suffer from epilepsy in America, and some would take marijuana if they could legally get it because it helps to control seizures," Steve Slater, a Texas-based advocate of marijuana legalization and a retired military engineer told me. "But often epileptics can't get access to it, such as in Arkansas. In fact, some epileptics have to move to different states that allow cannabis so they can get access to it. This moving sometimes results in breaking up families. It's ridiculous. An end to seizures shouldn't be determined by one's zip code."

America has undergone a prohibition era before from 1920 to 1933 with alcohol. Most people consider it a disaster. Not only did numerous distilleries appear selling illegal, untaxed, and unregulated drink, but alcohol prohibition grew to represent everything that was wrong with government. By the time Prohibition was lifted, many Americans thought their government was a joke. For millions of young people in the US, the feeling is the same regarding the War on Drugs.

Broadly a failure, the trillion dollar War on Drugs has done little to curb drug use, which remains common in just about every populated part of America. In fact, what the War on Drugs is best known for now is putting nonviolent offenders in jail. In 2014, media reported that every minute someone was arrested in the US for marijuana possession, totaling over 620,000 people. Costs associated with the arrests, processing, and incarceration were in the billions, and all of it taxpayer money.

"It's a medicine," said Morgan. "How can we be so closed-minded to arrest over a half-million Americans in a year for a medicine?"

To me, it's obvious that recreational drugs should be immediately legalized. Furthermore, those drugs should be taxed, and the money should be put into education. Colorado in an example of this. The $44 million dollar windfall that Colorado is enjoying this year from cannabis legalization is transforming its economy.

For me, Colorado has set the strong example that every state in America can benefit from marijuana. However, the more challenging question is whether all drugs should be legalized.

One European country, Portugal did this in 2001. A study done by the Cato Institute, the US-based libertarian think tank, showed that five years after this step, drug use among teens dropped and so did HIV infections caused by sharing needles.

Time Magazine reports:

"Judging by every metric, decriminalization in Portugal has been a resounding success," says Glenn Greenwald, an attorney, author and fluent Portuguese speaker, who conducted the research [yes, the same Greenwald who worked with Edward Snowden and broke the story of the US surveillance programs]. "It has enabled the Portuguese government to manage and control the drug problem far better than virtually every other Western country does."

Portugal, rather than spending its money on enforcing drug laws, spent those resources on rehabilitation of problem users.

It's the exact kind of idea that appeals to me, and based on Portugal's results, I'm willing to gently push for a totally free drug policy in America.

While a free-for-all on drugs in America may seem outrageous, there are more benefits to this than are obvious. Many prisons are filled with nonviolent drug offenders. We could let them go and save billions on prison costs for social services and education. And we need not let prisoners just go totally free either, but use radical drone technology to monitor them during their sentence time in the public.

Additionally, a free drug policy would have the benefit of lessening the power of the mafia, drug lords, and gangs who make black market money off selling substances. Maybe by legalizing drugs, we'd change the underground drug system enough that even black market players might start trying to build legitimate businesses and paying taxes.

"In the end of the day, drugs are about health and money," Morgan said. "And there's a lot of money to be made off of them. And that will benefit the economy—including both small and big businesses."

Despite my enthusiasm for legalizing most or even all drugs, I wouldn't want that to occur overnight. Care must be taken to work out the change that society would experience from such an important cultural shift. However, I do see the benefit of starting the conversation immediately to begin down that legalization road. I worry by being such a restrictive country as we are now, future generations will one day look back at us in ridicule, like how we look back at Prohibition. As a nation, it's time to move beyond the typical political and philosophical stance that recreational drug use is immoral. Instead, we should see drug use and experimentation as a positive endeavor a transhumanist society embraces to better itself.

****

13) Let's End Incarceration and Use Tech to Supervise Criminals

The US prison system costs almost four times more to run than the US education system. It doesn't matter what your politics are—virtually everyone thinks this is wrong. So what can we do about it?

As a transhumanist, I always look to science and technology to solve problems. The simple fact is that many criminals crowding our prisons—whether murders, drug dealers, or others—could be turned into law abiding, tax-paying citizens who live successfully amongst us. All they need is the proper supervision.

In the past, strict supervision like this has been impossible due to it being cost ineffective. There simply were not enough parole officers and police to monitor the plethora of criminals—approximately two million people are in US jails today. However, with new 21st century tech and tracking possibilities arriving, this may soon change.

Drones already cost less than $30 dollars. And using GPS directions, they'll soon be able to fly indefinitely based only on solar power and batteries. They will also soon be just the size of coins, like the Aerius made by Axis Drones. If every inmate was given a few tiny personal drones to follow them around, how much new crime do you think they would commit?

Generally speaking, criminals commit crimes when they think they can get away with it. So drones filming their every move and relaying images back to a sophisticated computer programmed to sense suspicious activity could majorly temper criminality.

Naturally, some felons would try to ditch their drones or smash them with a baseball bat. But since drones are becoming so cheap, perhaps we might always have a few spares hovering outside the house or wherever criminals go.

In fact, I would even advocate for every criminal having a full-sized robot guard personally assigned to them. While there are some sizeable upfront costs to this, eventually able-bodied robots will be able to be made affordably that can contain and apprehend criminals—and maybe even taser them in emergencies. In fact, South Korea has already implemented 5-foot robo-guards to help monitor criminals in their prisons.

If we add already existing interactive robot technology—where a live person, such a patrol officer, can see and hear through the robots' cameras and equipment—then we could control the robots as if they were our own bodies. These robot drones would indeed be a powerful force against crime without endangering the operator.

Of course, looking forward five years in the future, another sure way to keep an eye on criminals in the public is with tracking chip implants. Chip implants, which can already do various things in the body like test blood, would be useful in determining if a criminal was imbibing illegal drugs, which sometimes leads to criminal behavior.

Criminal chip implants would help with another problem prisons typically generate. While incarcerated, felons group together, and obviously this isn't very helpful in rehabilitating criminal attitudes. But in the outside world, a condition of freedom for felons might be the direct order not to associate with other criminals. This would force felons to be surrounded by noncriminal types. Peer pressure is a powerful force, and the ability to successfully intermix in society and contribute to the national best interest might be better achieved this way.

It's safe to say these new ideas of governing criminals would be far cheaper than the hugely expensive US prison system. How great would it be to get a majority of the two million prisoners in America into the workforce and paying taxes again? In fact, with all that money earned (and saved), we could finally start to spend money building out this country's inadequate education system. We might even consider using the thousands of empty prisons around the country as part of a new national university system that offers college education to anyone that wants it. By freeing prisoners, we could end up hiring thousands of new teachers.

Opportunities abound for prison reform, but it starts with a close look at how improving technology could lead to much less incarceration in the first place.

****

14) How Technology Could Facilitate and then Destroy Immigration

Immigration—it's one of the hot button topics of the elections. Republican Donald Trump wants to build a huge wall between the US and Mexico. Democrats was to make it easier for immigrants to come to America. The presidential candidates' opinions on immigration and its effect on America are essentially polar opposites.

Despite this, neither Trump or the Democrats are talking about the issue that could redefine immigration more than anything else in the next quarter century: technology. Surveillance tech, facial recognition software, drones, and chip implants are all here—and becoming more commonplace. Their use in who we let into America—and how we let them in—will play a big part of immigration in the future.

For example, Trump's wall between Mexico and the United States—designed to thwart illegal immigration—is estimated to cost upwards of $25 billion dollars. It'll probably never get built, and even if it did, its effectiveness is highly questionable. Walls can be scaled, or tunnels can be dug underneath.

For a pittance of the money his wall will cost, American border patrol could buy and use thousands of drones that day and night monitor our borders. Drones can have loud bilingual speakers to talk to illegal immigrants trying to cross into America, and they can also have facial recognition software to see if immigrants are on criminal lists. A tight line of small camera drones at the nearly 2,000 mile long US/Mexico border seems much more practical than a wall—especially with coming AI that can simultaneously monitor and manage all the drones at once. Along the border, inexpensive charging stations could be set up where drones recharge themselves as needed.

Additionally, drones would be far better for wildlife and nature near the border than a massive concrete wall. A wall would require much construction equipment, human traffic, and newly built roads to create (and to maintain). Wildlife near the border would suffer because their feeding, living, and hunting grounds had been cut in half and disrupted. Drones and their occasional charging stations will disrupt far less and leave nearly no footprint.

Most importantly, drones can save lives too. They can spot children being trafficked, harmful drugs or weapons being brought across the border, or dehydrated immigrants who need immediate medical assistance. New unmanned passenger drones like those being created by Chinese entrepreneurs might help with medical evacuations.

The idea of dealing with refugees—another form of immigration—is much more difficult to contend with. In 2013, the number of immigrants granted permanent resident status was 990,553. Refugees—many of whom are from war zones—make up less than 100,000 of that number. The US often provides cash and housing for refugees, which comes from taxpayers.

Many Republican and some Democrat Congress members don't want war refugees here. And more than half of state governors don't want them in their states either. The numbers tell the full story: America has plans to only let in 10,000 Syrian refugees this year versus Germany which has already let in nearly a million total. Germany is about a quarter of the size of America in population.

As a journalist who has been to war zones, I believe in giving refugees sanctuary, especially to women, children, the disabled, and the elderly. However, I don't believe in allowing them into America without some special surveillance or giving them a free ride year after year. Some seemingly authoritative measures should be administered.

I have suggested we have a discussion about chipping adult refugees from known terrorist nations for the first three years of their stay in America to better monitor them. This way, we can allay terrorism concerns, and we can make sure refugees are adding to American life—and not harming it.

Chip implants in the hand, for example, take seconds to install and seconds to uninstall. And they can be used for a multitude of things, like making credit card payments, carrying valuable information, starting a car without keys, and tracking purposes.

While some will believe this is authoritarian, I believe half of Americans will get some type of implant or tattoo chip to facilitate tech functionality in their lives in the next decade (besides getting recognized by AI using facial recognition). So getting the ball rolling with refugees from known terrorist countries is not as intense as it sounds—especially if it makes Congress members more compassionate about letting them into America. *And* that is the main point with chipping refugees—that it might just be the carrot both Republican and Democrat Congress members need to pass laws to save hundreds of thousands of lives by allowing wartorn refugees into the US. If we don't create an acceptable bipartisan scenario where we let in refugees, then millions of innocent human beings will continue to be killed and harmed in totally destroyed cities and warzones.

But there's a far more complex issue with immigration looming on the horizon: The proliferation of robots and the jobs they take will challenge why we allow immigrants into the country in the first place.

As a political candidate who was born in Los Angeles but is both the son of immigrants and a dual citizen (Hungary), I believe in the concept of immigration. Immigrants—like my parents who escaped communist Hungary in 1969—come to America for many reasons, but mostly it has to do with building a better life and finding a good job.

The same thing can be said of nations that let in immigrants—they too want to build a better life for their citizens and get better workers. Generally speaking, nations that allow immigrants into their society do so not to be generous, but because immigrants are useful for the growth and prosperity of the nation.

In the past century, it's been useful to allow most anyone into America that would work, pay taxes, and not commit crimes. However, in a world where jobs are disappearing to robots and software, there's less need than ever for immigrants—unless they happen to be robot makers or software engineers.

This presents a conundrum for the world. Because I support a Universal Basic Income (UBI)—where every citizen gets a livable income whether they work or not—I know that immigration for citizenship privileges in America will eventually have to drop to near zero. Otherwise America will have to merge with other nations to create a UBI everywhere—since everyone would want to immigrate to America for the free money.

The UBI concept is catching on with many people around the world, as well as in Silicon Valley, where many robots are being designed. There's a general feeling that something needs to be done to stave off a people's potentially violent revolution if most jobs are consumed by technology and machines.

One idea, which I gently support, is greater cooperation of national governments. Despite the shock of Brexit, a loose form of a democratic world government is likely inevitable over the long run. Technology will make it such that globalization is the optimal style of governing, and not nationalism.

The flip side to not embracing globalization and increased cooperation between nations is to let tech create a dystopian divide where the rich become wealthier and the poor poorer. Globalization and world-wide laws, benefits, and cultural unity are the key to equality.

One main difference of such a scenario would be immigration. While I would likely support open borders in a world government (and support some versions of open borders now), some people might not want to leave their native lands if there was a livable wage to be had there. Others might move, but they'd have the guaranteed resources to contribute and participate in society.

Strangely enough, it's even possible that technology may someday be on the receiving end of immigration, where robots and artificial intelligences (possibly even with personhood rights) from China or Germany have to undergo immigration clearances in order to be able to operate in America. And some of this tech might be so sophisticated (or so poor in performance) that they wouldn't be allowed in at all—because they'd create a perceived economic disruption to the economy and status quo.

Whatever happens, the way we look at immigration is about to undergo major changes because of technology. Through it all, we must maintain both a sense of compassion to people's quest for a better life, and a sense of rationality for economic and security decisions of national governments trying to deal with the thorny situation of newcomers (and new tech) permanently entering their societies

****

15) Space Exploration will Spur Transhumanism and Mitigate Existential Risk

When people think about rocket ships and space exploration, they often imagine traveling across the Milky Way, landing on mysterious planets and even meeting alien life forms.

In reality, humans' drive to get off Planet Earth has led to tremendous technological advances in our mundane daily lives — ones we use right here at home on terra firma.

I recently walked through Boston's Logan International Airport; a NASA display reminded me that GPS navigation, anti-icing systems, memory foam and LED lights were all originally created for space travel. Other inventions NASA science has created include the pacemaker, scratch-resistant lenses and the solar panel.

These types of advancements are one of the most important reasons I am hoping our next U.S. president will try to jump-start the American space program — both privately and publicly. Unfortunately, it doesn't appear any of them are talking about the issue in a serious way. But they should be. As we enter the transhumanist age — the era of bionic limbs, brain implants and artificial intelligence — space exploration might once again dramatically lead us forward in discovering the most our species can become.

Already SpaceX, led by CEO Elon Musk, has announced it will be tackling an unmanned trip to Mars in the near future. The hope, of course, is that within the next 10 years, astronauts will be stepping foot upon the red planet, too. If indeed, humans can make it to Mars — and I'm sure we will — much new tech would have to be developed for the mission. It's safe to say much of that tech would likely be something useful for us eventually on Earth, as well.

For example, just to even live in space for the journey — it'll take approximately six months to travel one-way to Mars — new ways of sleeping, recycling breathable air and preserving foods and drink would likely have to be developed.

Furthermore, the technology to withstand massive dust storms, freezing temperatures and a hostile environment on Mars would require new space suits and maybe even totally new materials. Innovation like this will benefit everyone — even if we don't know all the uses yet for such radical tech.

Of course, there are other reasons for prompting a renewed and significantly larger space program in America. One of the fundamental goals of my own presidential campaign has been warning the world of the incredible threat of existential risk.

The Atlantic recently ran a story by Robinson Meyer that read: At life-long scales, one in 120 Americans die in an accident. The risk of human extinction due to climate change — or an accidental nuclear war — is much higher than that. *The Stern Review*, the U.K.

government's premier report on the economics of climate change, estimated a 0.1 percent risk of human extinction every year. That may sound low, but it also adds up when extrapolated to century-scale. Across 100 years, that figure would entail a 9.5 percent chance of human extinction.

I think most people are totally unaware at how high the odds are that we screw up our species' very existence. It's so high, that the newly written *Transhumanist Bill of Rights* has a mandate for space exploration as one of its key six points.

The facts of existential risk are simple: We may not be able to indefinitely keep the planet habitable, stop a super virus from killing everyone, avoid a mile-wide asteroid from crashing into Earth, elude a warmongering Terminator-like AI or circumvent blowing ourselves up with our 25,000 nuclear warheads — but we sure can get off this planet and create cool new places to live safely in outer space.

The movie Elysium recently showed a dystopic but technologically plausible space habitat, where paradise is engineered in the skies — and not on Earth's land or water. Now, no one wants to be forced into this scenario, but massive space habitats are worthwhile projects to pursue — and they could be possible to build in as little as 15 years.

Mega-space habitats would also make an easier launch base for space mining, an industry booming with interest. Experts say it will soon be possible to mine asteroids from space — some that are worth billions of dollars each. Clive Thomson at *Wired* recently wrote that the asteroid Ryugu — partially made of up of nickel, iron and cobalt — could be worth up to $95 billion.

As a science advocate, I'm strongly pro-space exploration from a private industry point of view. But just as importantly, I also passionately support a U.S. government-sponsored space program — one that gets approximately 10 times the funding it gets now (I'd get that extra money from our military budget, which is oversized anyway). That would be nearly $100 billion a year, or about 5 percent of the U.S. 2016 Federal budget.

Generally, my fiscally-minded self doesn't want the government too involved in much of anything, but because space exploration involves defending against existential risk and pursuing medical innovation for citizens, I'd advocate for the U.S. putting dramatically more resources into space exploration. This wouldn't mean entirely relying on federal programs to push forward the space industry, but also on government partnering with or investing in private space companies.

Sadly, Congress will likely put up a fight against spending too much on peacetime space exploration — they do have that habit of being boring and shortsighted. So, perhaps the best way to grow America's space industry is to sell Congress on the amount of benefits our nation might gain from a meaningful and dramatically enlarged space program. Generally, politicians — those directly responsible for funding (or not funding) NASA — see no upside for sending astronauts to space except national pride.

But if Congress could be convinced that national security against existential risk, money from space mining, and precious tech innovation for U.S. citizens would be gained by supporting space exploration, then maybe they would vote to enlarge NASA's programs. This in turn would spur both the private space industry as well as transhumanism tech that makes all our lives better. This type of thinking should be a priority for whoever ends up in Congress and the White House this next election.

****

16) Is it Time for a Transhumanist Olympics?

Oracle Team USA made a historic comeback to beat Emirates Team New Zealand in the American's Cup in San Francisco Bay in 2013. I have closely followed the sport of sail racing for over 30 years, and what astonishes me is how much faster and better the boats are today than they were three decades ago. Sailing speeds and performances have doubled in some cases.

The same cannot be said about most other major sports. Even Michael Phelps, considered by many the greatest living athlete, is only a few seconds faster than swimming world records set 30 years ago. Most sports have not allowed scientific improvements or technology upgrades to their athletes and the equipment they use. I find that disappointing.

What is on the rise in athletics, however, are multi-million dollar campaigns and testing measures designed to ensure athletes don't cheat by using performance enhancing drugs and technologies. Some athletes even complain about undergoing TSA-like testing procedures right before their events. Does anyone else see a problem with that? Does anyone else see something anti-progressive about the state of our competitive sporting industry today?

As an advanced society full of technological wonders, perhaps it's time we consider upgrading our idea of sports and rethinking what constitutes an exemplary athlete. Perhaps it's time for something more modern and exciting, such as the transhuman athlete.

Transhumanism is a broad term that means beyond human. The word often incorporates many different ideas, including those of radical life extension science, genetic engineering, bionics, and anything else that makes the human being more advanced than our everyday 21st Century Homo sapiens.

In the last 50 years, science and technology have brought our society into a new age. Whether it's the internet, space travel, or the harnessing of nuclear energy, the world is a very different place than when the first modern-day Olympics took place in 1896 in Greece.

Rather than change traditional sporting events, which hold a special place in many of our hearts, why not add a whole new category to them? For a moment, imagine a transhumanist Olympic Games: a place for athletes in the 21st Century who have modified themselves with drugs, technologies, and bionic enhancements. A place where the best human potential combines with the most advanced science to create the coolest competitions possible. Who wouldn't be thrilled to be at an Olympics where humans can pole vault over 25 meters? Or peddle a bicycle 150 miles per hour? Or powerlift a ton.

"Multiple medical and surgical technologies already exist to improve physical performance," says Dr. Joseph N. Carey, a plastic and reconstructive surgeon at University of Southern California Keck

School of Medicine. "These technologies can be used to maximize, or even supercharge human abilities. The question is: Will society ever begin to think implementing such actions is a good thing?"

Some might call scientifically enhanced athletes mutants. Many futurists, scientists, and technologists, however, would call them inspirational heroes, leading the way forward to discover how far the human body can be made to perform. Instead of developing a culture of paranoia at athletes using illegal technologies and performance enhancing drugs, why not develop a culture where athleticism can be combined with the most advanced science on the planet? Let coaches get advanced degrees in biology, chemistry, and medicine. Let entire new industries emerge which are dedicated to improving athletic performance via the latest tech. Let a whole new genre of sporting events develop. Let a new category of athletes become the very best in their sports that they can become.

We've never limited the car, plane, or boat from performing as mightily as it could. Why should we limit the human body? I don't approve of Lance Armstrong, Marion Jones, and Mark McGwire for lying to us, but I do applaud them for attempting to be better at their sports via outside resources.

Many will say performance enhancing drugs and technologies are dangerous and will shorten competitive athletes' life spans. That may be true, but who are we to make that decision for them? For some, the passion of their sport and the glory of their performance are the most important things in life to them. Should we really have a say in how far they want to take their passion for the game?

Of course, such a transition to transhumanist sports would need to be regulated. Persons under a minimum age, such as 18 years-old, should not be allowed to engage in major body modifications for athleticism. Nor should the casual athlete use known dangerous drugs as way to enhance their play. Yet, as an advanced scientific-minded civilization, it makes sense to encourage a select group of super-athletes to inspire us with their unnatural strength, speed, and performances.

There's something else to be benefited from pursuing the emergence of transhumanist sports. Athletes would explore new technologies and drugs for the benefit of us all. Such a multi-billion dollar field as competitive sports could lead to new discoveries in the medical sciences. These transhumanist competitors could become our fire-bearers—our Prometheuses carrying the torch from Mount Olympus.

Our civilization has reached its impressive dominion over the planet because of our ability to innovate and embrace new science and technologies. We shouldn't shrug from the use of our innovation on ourselves. We especially shouldn't shrug from the use of 21st Century science and technology on a select group of our very best athletes who we follow and admire.

****

17) How to End Taxes Forever

It's said that nothing is for sure but death and taxes. Anti-aging scientists are already working on getting rid of death, but what about taxes? If we all live thousands of years, will we also have to pay the IRS every April 15th?

It's unlikely. Individual income taxes will not survive the end of the century, if they even survive the next few decades, due to the coming robot and 3D printing revolution.

In little more than 20 years, about 75 percent of all jobs and occupations will be severely challenged by robots and software—both of which will be able to do jobs better and cheaper than humans. And by the end of the century, it's possible that basically all jobs may be replaced by unmanned machines.

However, it's not because humans won't be working that we may no longer pay taxes—after all, money and consumerism aren't going anywhere soon. But paying taxes generally is related to government spending. And governments will certainly continue to spend money, but not the people's money. Rather they will spend resources they create and control—like robot power. They will do this in the same way they print money on demand and control interest rates as needed to keep economies moving along smoothly.

In the future, when government needs more worker power to implement policy, it will just put in orders for more bots at factories it controls—giant 3D printing facilities. The CIA Headquarters, US Congress, and even the White House will likely have their own robot creation facilities ready to produce on-demand a plethora of functional machines they need.

All this sounds a bit fanciful. But a deeper look into the future of economics shows us why so many radical changes are imminent.

To begin with, there's really only two ways for America to proceed in our transhuman future. We can kill the robot revolution by saying no to robots taking our jobs—frankly, this will never happen, since a critical component of 21st century economics is corporations continually modernizing to make or save more money. Or we can embrace robots, and begin the strange path to a world where humans don't work and machines do everything for us. Yes, it will eventually be the end of capitalism as we know it, but economic competition will still survive a while. It just won't be borne on the back of humans, but on machines.

If this all sounds impossible, consider that countries are already testing driverless trucks on the road to deliver goods. In the United States, there were 1.7 million heavy and tractor-trailer truck drivers in 2014, according to the Bureau of Labor Statistics, and most of those drivers cannot be easily trained to do other jobs. What do they do when they get replaced? Trucking is just one of dozens of industries over the next five years that will run head-on into the robot revolution.

Society must soon come to grips with the fact that nearly all human employment is susceptible to extinction in the next few decades. While this might frighten some, I support robots taking our jobs, as I think it will usher in a new American Dream, one that doesn't include working the 9 to 5 grind, but having time for oneself to do whatever.

For me, the key to a new American Dream is the Universal Basic Income (UBI). To keep progress and economies moving forward, it's okay to replace human workers with machines, but we must compensate people adequately and indefinitely. Where does that money come from? First from the $200 trillion dollars of Federal

Land the government owns and can lease out or sell. The other answer is that robots will make industries so much efficient that there will be ample money—probably via higher corporate taxes from higher profits—to dish out a livable income to replaced workers. Though, I'm not a fan of higher taxes and prefer to let abundant natural resources do the job.

Interestingly, corporate taxes will also likely disappear in the long run, as new technologies and engineering innovation methods become more valuable than money and are required by government to manage populations. Corporations will help their government out by sharing technology, not by paying taxes.

However, most importantly, with a UBI, individuals paying taxes will be totally phased out, since there will be no money created by people. In fact, welfare and social security will also end, as a UBI will totally replace the need for it, thereby further shrinking the government.

Historically, Americans didn't always pay taxes, anyway. Income tax only arrived permanently in America in 1913. Over time, the US government ratcheted up income taxes, sales taxes, property taxes, and other types. Today, we are drowning in taxes, due to one single factor—the government needs more money than ever to operate. But an automated government will not need money. It will need more robots to operate and implement control and defense—and it will need more robots to program code to create more sophisticated unmanned machines for its endless use.

The key factor here is that at some point in the future, the government will only need its own robot factories, which it will build. The government doesn't need to acquire natural resources to build things, since it already has plenty of them—it owns over half the resource-rich land in 11 Western states, including mineral, oil, timber, water rights and more.

All the American government really needs now is the public to vote in good representatives who can understand and utilize technology to govern better. And with that better management will come the technological-inspired extinction of all personal taxes—and freedom from the Uncle Sam.

18) Mass Shootings and Terrorism can be Stopped by Drones, Robots, and AI Scanners

Every time a mass shooting occurs in America, gun owners and supporters are blamed for the tragic violence. The Parkland school shooting in Florida was no different. Gun control advocates immediately began calling for stricter gun control laws in America. They won't get far, though: More than 300 million guns are floating around our 50 states, and the number is unlikely to be reduced anytime soon, whether by law or not.

Might there be another way to have so-called "gun control" and still have the freedom to have 300 million or more guns? The answers lie in radical technology. In the recent Las Vegas massacre, a lone shooter from the 32nd floor of a hotel room shot and killed 58 people over approximately 10 minutes at a nearby music festival before police could stop him. Had an armed police drone—or at least a security drone with a smoke bomb or flares—been able to get to the shooter's broken hotel windows from the music venue, dozens of lives might've have been saved. The distance from the shooter to the victims was only about 300 yards. Drones can fly 120 miles per hour and could have likely reached the shooter's room in less than 30 seconds.

Using GPS and custom AI algorithms that detect gunfire bursts and explosion sounds from weapons, a waiting police drone could have found and confronted the shooter in probably less than a minute. It could have exploded a nonlethal smoke bomb in the room of the shooter or directly attacked the shooter himself with weapons.

Drones can also be led to exact locations to stop shooters by specialized smoke alarms that sense gun smoke, sending out GPS coordinates to where the shooting is coming from, or they could be notified through smart building technology built into windows and doors that notify authorities when they've been tampered with or broken. The Las Vegas shooter broke two of his hotel room windows to shoot out of, but no one knew until the shooting began.

Much of this technology is essentially here, and the U.S. military is on the cutting edge with its armada of drones and drone tech. Citizens that desire gun control ought to instead insist the government ask its drone-making partners like Boeing, Lockheed Martin, and other contractors to their products into public protection devices—rather than using them for far-off wars. Even better, private companies like GoPro could help jumpstart the personal security field of drones to help halt terrorism and mass shootings in America.

In the future, all public spaces, schools, and events should consider having terrorism-deterrent drones to protect its citizens—both inside and outdoors. This kind of protection is culturally and institutionally no different than a fire alarm, a fire extinguisher, and the fire department—something that dates back two centuries in America. Even liberty-minded people like myself can get behind it.

Beyond drones, there's gun-surveillance technology. Already, police have the ability to see through walls. Why don't public spaces and schools have special viewing technology that easily registers metal-shaped objects from afar? It's not that hard for a special camera or electromagnetic sensor to detect a hidden metal L-shaped handgun-like object or a long metal rifle in a duffle bag. If a weapon is detected in the camera or sensor, it could send a message to a computer to sound the alarm to alert security and electronically lock doors, whether on a campus or in a place of business or government building. The alarm could also immediately notify authorities and launch that newly acquired security drone to check out and possibly stop an imminent tragedy. Some companies are working on this already, and major casinos in Las Vegas are now experimenting with electromagnetic gun surveillance technology in their lobbies.

People are rightfully distressed at being spied upon and the use of surveillance tech, especially since it's becoming so powerful and pervasive. But a modified thermal camera or electromagnetic sensor need not be able to identify people or their faces. Rather, it could be programmed to only detect weapons and nothing else.

The gun control question in America has been escalating in intensity for decades. It's true that there are about as many gun deaths as driving deaths now, which is unfortunate. I believe something should be done about it—and that something involves gun control. But the control need not come from limiting sales and ownership of guns, but rather from limiting criminals being able to carry out violence in public or private spaces. That can best be done by innovative technology—some of which already exists and much more of which can be quickly developed.

****

19) A Federal Land Dividend Could Provide a Universal Basic Income

The US government owns over $150 trillion of federal land and resources. Most of it is unused and sitting idle. If you divide $150 trillion by America's 325 million citizens, you get nearly a half-million dollars per person.

If the US could just figure out how to monetize that federal land and distribute its equity equally, Americans could forever overcome poverty, healthcare issues, and the impending "robocalypse" — where increasing automation replaces tens of millions of human jobs.

As a political candidate, I've been racking my brain to come up with a bipartisan plan to improve the American financial landscape and stop worsening inequality.

I knew the key rested in America's vast untapped wealth of federal land, which is valued at over six times our national debt. But in order to monetize this land, it would have to be sold or leased out to private businesses that can use it.

Rightfully so, most Americans do not want to sell the country's forests, lakes, fossil fuel reserves, and other assets off forever. The next best thing, then, is of course, leasing it out. Leasing out federal land could provide a permanent regular income to every American, without giving up ownership of the land. I call this idea a Federal Land Dividend, and it's the first plausible universal basic income plan that doesn't raise taxes or target the rich — which is why I believe Congress will be interested in it.

The Federal Land Dividend works like this: It issues out leases anywhere from 25 years to 99 years. Companies would offer bids for land and resources they wanted, and binding lease agreements would be created. I'm guessing most leases would be structured around a standard 5% annual interest rate, plus inflation when necessary.

If 85% of $150 trillion of federal land was leased out — which would allow all national parks and their 80 million acres to remain untouched (something I would insist on) — then every American, regardless of age, would receive $20,000 a year, or $1,700 a month indefinitely.

When the typical American household of four people combines that amount, it then becomes $80,000 annually per household. That's quite far above the current median US household income of $52,000, and it's plenty for families to live on in nearly every part of America. And naturally, personal incomes would add to what the Federal Land Dividend provided.

Just about anyone will accept free money. But the strongest opposition to the Federal Land Dividend comes from environmentalists. They go bonkers at the thought of America's pristine lands and waters being commercialized.

I believe we ought to try to respect those opinions, and the way to do this is two-fold: Leave national parks alone. Second: make all leases contain a clause that requires companies to leave the land and environment just as they found it when their lease is over— something that will be made easier in the future with coming nanotechnology and geoengineering.

Environmentalists will probably still find a reason not to be happy with the plan, but they must remember that the Federal Land Dividend's goal is to eliminate poverty and increase equality. Currently, 13 million American kids go to bed hungry at night and approximately 1.5 million people will be homeless in the US at some point in 2017. Our country's assets — the land and its resources that belongs to the people — should be used for the health and security of its citizens.

Besides, there is a huge national and global threat on the horizon America must prepare for: robots taking most human jobs. Over the next five years, it's likely machines will replace millions of human jobs in the US. For example, recently, McDonald's stock reached an all-time high as investors cheered automated ordering kiosks replacing cashiers.

The threat is real, and the Federal Land Dividend provides an indefinite income that American families can live and thrive on, whether they're employed or not.

Another reason the Federal Land Dividend may be welcomed is because it solves a number of longstanding American dilemmas, like the possibility that Social Security will one day be insolvent. The Federal Land Dividend can replace Social Security outright. It could also replace welfare, food stamp programs, and the endless debate about how to provide affordable healthcare in this country. A major reason I support the Federal Land Dividend is it will finally allow all people to afford health insurance they need—essentially accomplishing the same as universal health coverage but through private means.

A basic income simplifies life while also protecting it. That's why billionaire CEOs like Facebook's Mark Zuckerberg and Tesla's Elon Musk support the idea of basic income. Done properly, it's a bipartisan plan that benefits both rich and poor.

The American Dream used to be about working hard and achieving the good life. Our predecessors did so well that America is now the greatest, most prosperous nation on the planet. We have the resources to give every American the good life. Now we just must embark on a mission to monetize those resources and distribute them to each American.

****

CHAPTER III: IDEAS THAT CHALLENGE

20) The Transhumanist Party's Founder on the Future of Politics

As the chairman of the Transhumanist Party, I often get asked about the long term future of politics. Frankly, it's a daunting subject. Looking forward 25 years and trying to gauge how rapidly advancing technology is going to change the nature of governance is a difficult, variable-filled prospect.

Technology, after all, is rapidly changing just about every area of human endeavor. Healthcare is morphing into cyborg-care, where doctor visits sometimes include software updates. New sports like Zorb racing or Speed Riding, a combination of paragliding and skiing, are born all the time. Even travel is on the verge of some possible colossal shifts with driverless cars and projects like the Hyperloop.

But what about politics? Just about everyone on the planet directly participates in politics, and has strong opinions about government. Will politics as it stands, with its voting booths, hand-waiving candidates, and rowdy national conventions remain the same as the transhumanist age thoroughly engulfs us? Or will government itself change in form as digital-everything becomes the norm?

Take virtual reality for example. It's likely, especially after Facebook's purchase of the Oculus Rift, that an increasing amount of people will be immersed in VR worlds within the next five to ten years. It's possible that an entire mirror civilization of our species will appear in VR, one that will surely be more welcome for some than our current reality, as is sometimes the case in Second Life.

But who will monitor this expanding VR world? Does it belong to national governments? Right now it does, but what if someone creates a VR world that shoots its signal from space, as some entrepreneurs want to do? Will that virtual world belong to Earth? Or to the company that created it? Or to the person that created it, who might declare themselves emperor or cult leader of their worlds.

Such ideas are not as far-fetched as they seem. There are already a number of movements and organizations afoot in the physical world to bring about stateless societies. The better ones tend to have extensive manifestos and hold egalitarian values. One group is Zero State, and its basic idea is to create networks of people and resources which could evolve into a distributed, virtual state. They currently have a few thousand members. Bitnation is another virtual nation, and they seek to use Blockchain tech to create laws and help with jurisdiction issues.

Additionally, the Transhumanist Party Virtual was recently formed, which aims to unite and support the many national transhumanist political parties that have recently popped up.

Is it possible that in the future, the state as we know it might not exist? To be sure, we'd need much more radical technology for such an idea to even be realistically feasible. But experts say some of that technology is coming. Recently, Jose Cordeiro, a Singularity University professor, told a crowd at the World Future Society that spoken language "could start disappearing in 15 years."

He thinks mindreading headsets may replace spoken language and significantly improve human communications. In the past, I've written about how these mindreading headsets will make future music concerts virtual, and how they will also likely reduce the need for knowing a second language, since something like Google translator will make on-demand translations for people. In short, everyone on the planet will understand everyone else—all the time. And this could start being our main communication in as little as two decades.

When you think about it, the planet could become a lot smaller very quickly if we could get over the language barrier that eight billion people have with each other. Furthermore, it's likely those mindreading headsets won't even be headsets in 20 years. They'll be chip implants in our heads, and despite everyone's complaints about over-surveillance, such implants will simply be too useful not to have. Everyone will have an implant, and they'll monitor everything about our lives, including our health, well being, and safety.

If I had to guess (and mind you, I'm not advocating for this, but just telling you how I see it playing out), I'm betting that many, if not most, countries will merge in the 21st century as a digital-inspired globalization further takes root. I'm betting one central virtual currency will be used too—maybe even Bitcoin if it can get over some of its many birthing hiccups. I'm betting borders will fall away and people will be able to travel, work, and live wherever they want. In general, rules and barriers don't help prosperity in the long term, but freedom and technology do.

So how might such a global government operate? It's possible in the future, should we all be so interconnected, that one central agency will virtually send out items for everyone to vote on—called a Direct Digital Democracy. Maybe there will be one special day of the year where all major voting and decisions take place. Possibly, smaller policies will be implemented on a rolling basis as they get enough people to consider and support them. That's democracy in real time—and we should expect that in the future too.

The wildcard here is AI, and the rise of an Artificial General Intelligence that rivals our own. Right about at the same time, in approximately 20 years, when we'll be reaching many technologies that will be transformative for the human species—such as ubiquitous telepathy between people—we'll also be launching AI. In its first year of existence, AI could become much, much smarter than us—10,000 times smarter than us, even. I tend to believe, like most everyone else, that AI must be carefully regulated so it doesn't create a Terminator-like scenario for the planet. But I'm also confident we can create an AI that will help our species indefinitely. Which brings us to the obvious question: Should we let AI run the government once it's smarter than us? Take that one step further— should we let that AI be the President—maybe even giving it a robot form for aesthetics or familiarity's sake?

It's not that bizarre of a concept. Who didn't watch Deep Blue beat Kasparov in Chess and wonder if a new age of intellect had arrived—one that was quite different than our own?

In Arthur C. Clarke's science fiction novel *Childhood's End*, aliens take over the world and inspire humanity to live peacefully and productively. The world experiences a golden age of prosperity. Perhaps AI policies would do the same thing. We would have government and a leader who really is after the world's best interests, free from the hazards of corporate lobbyists and selfishness.

As a futurist and a political candidate, a central aim of mine is to do the most good for the greatest amount of people. I still find the AI rulership scenario a hard pill to swallow. I love my freedoms, win or lose, more that infinite productivity. But perhaps as technology engulfs us, and we grow less afraid of losing our freedoms and more appreciative of all our uber-modern benefits, we'll feel differently—especially as we all experience near-perfect health, unprecedented safety, and a utopian, transhumanist existence.

****

21) In the Age of Longer Lifespans, Should College be Mandatory?

Regardless what state you live in, at least some high school education or its equivalent is required by law in America. These mandates ensure most every kid enters adulthood with the skills to read, write, perform mathematics, and be moderately civilized.

But in an era where scientists believe people born today may live to 150 years of age, are we shortchanging ourselves by not requiring a longer, more rigorous period of education for our youth? Is kindergarten to high school really sufficient for centenarians, or is it time to require all American kids start attending college too?

The history of compulsory education in America goes back almost a century. By 1918, every state required kids to attend at least elementary school. Over the following nine decades, states increased their educational requirements, ensuring youth continue their schooling until at least until 15 years of age, but often until 17 or 18. Whether by traditional high school, charter school, or home schooling, in the 21st century the majority of American youth—almost 80 percent—graduate with a high school-level education.

Most of us take this all for granted because education is so enshrined in American culture and social life. Receiving some form of schooling seems to be the one major topic that citizens—regardless of politics, race, ethnicity, religion, and wealth—agree is positive. A lot of this is due to the fact that education improves one's odds of succeeding in the job market. However, that job market is changing quickly. Last decade, the big news was jobs moving overseas to China. Now it's machines taking many of the jobs in America that are left. Experts predict that by 2025 a third of all jobs will be lost to robots and software.

Politicians are fumbling over themselves trying to find a way to stop this job-loss carnage, one that is a real threat to many US citizens. There's no easy answer to the problem, but one thing is for sure, getting everyone to attend college probably can't hurt. It's a well-known fact that higher education generally makes one far more likely to be employed, get better wages, and land the job and career they want. Studies have shown college grads are happier, healthier, remain married longer, and end up considerably wealthier later in life than those who stopped their educations directly after high school.

In fact, if you look closely, it's hard to find any downsides of receiving a higher education at all. Most people are genuinely in favor of the idea of our country spilling over with spunky, self-confident college grads looking to change the world. The promise of discussing Noam Chomsky, String Theory, and Moore's Law with any twenty-something-year-old you meet on the street seems refreshing.

Of course, college is about much more than just scholastic education. It's also about interacting with professors, debating peers over controversial books, and choosing a worthy major. For many, college also goes hand in hand with wild parties, foreign travel, drugs, new philosophies, and sexual exploration. It's no wonder many people call college the best years of their lives.

So why doesn't society legally mandate such a universally positive experience? Why do we stop at high school and leave the main course of educational development on the table, untouched?

Part of the problem has to do with lifespans. Between the 1920s and 1960s when many states passed the bulk of their compulsory high school education laws, lifespans averaged about 63 years of age.

That left an 18-year-old high school grad with paltry 35 years to find a spouse, have babies, make a career, and get prepared for a decade long retirement before dying.

What a difference a few generations make. Most youth today expect to live to at least 100. Marriage is in slow decline. Retirement seems boring. And increasingly men and women are seeing IVF culture as a safeguard to push back having children until their late 30s. All this leaves much more time for pursuits like travel, professional ambitions, education, and even just simple loafing. Extended longevity and advancing reproductive science are wonderful things, but they're really just the tip of the iceberg. In the future, expect these trends to sharply accelerate, giving both women and men much more time in their 20s and 30s to figure out what they want to do in life.

Here lies the real conundrum with upcoming generations. With all this extra free time, doesn't it make sense to require our youth to educate themselves more? It will only help them figure themselves out more and give them the skills to reach whatever dreams they want. Unfortunately, the problems with such a proposal are deep and multifaceted. For starters, such a proposal reeks of authoritarianism. It's understandable to demand 17-year-old go to school. But a 21-year old who is already a bonafide tax paying adult? Compliance with such a law might be impossible. College dropout rates could soar. Our culture has long established that once a kid hits 18 and is out of high school, they are a free agent—a master of the universe.

Another issue critics will have is the complaint that mandating higher education will mean the Mark Zuckerbergs and Tiger Woods of the world won't be able to start their companies or turn pro in their sports, since they'll be forced to go to school. An easy way around that dilemma is to create a college equivalent test, similar to the high school GED. Kids that are smart enough to pass can skip out on school if they don't want to go. They'll miss out on the fun, but at least society will know they've got the smarts to succeed.

The biggest issue about compulsory higher education, though, is affordability: Who is going to pay for almost 20 million American youth to go to college? You won't convince an entire generation of students to take out loans. America is already facing a serious school loan crisis. Maybe, society could incentivize attending college. Might we pay students to get an upper education, like some places in Europe? Or what about offering significant tax benefits, or even creating a monster sister-bill to the existing GI Bill? We might also consider monetizing America's vast Federal Land to pay for it.

One important idea for me could involve lessening prison operation costs across America. According to a recent report, we spend four times the amount on the American prison system than on education. Many convicts are between 18-22 years of age. Perhaps college would keep them out of prison and significantly drop incarceration and judicial costs. It might be enough to help foot a compulsory college education bill while also improving crime rates around the country.

As challenging as financial considerations for all this might be, the flipside of the coin and its liabilities might be more daunting. In an age where jobs are being lost to machines and China may already be academically our superior, perhaps America needs to dig deeper into its pockets to make its kids smarter. Perhaps the more important question is: In order to protect our future and our nation, can we afford not to have all our youth receive some higher education?

It's worth mentioned too that getting a college education is no longer exclusively living in dorms and learning in brick and mortar classrooms, many of which are halfway across the country. Education is moving online in a big way; virtual classrooms are popping up everywhere. Already, almost all higher education institutions, from small liberal arts colleges to the Ivy League, now offer online classes. Many future students might not even need to leave their homes to get a bachelor's degree. Online education is generally far cheaper than attending a traditional college, and this could significantly help with compulsory upper education costs.

America is entering one of the most challenging times it's ever faced. We are up against increasing wealth inequality, frightening climate issues, and growing technological dominance over nearly every aspect of our lives. Are we going to shortchange our youth because we can't afford it? Or because it's too bossy of us? Or because it requires going against decades of institutionalized culture. Perhaps it's time to ante up: Build new colleges. Hire new teachers. Forge new curriculums. And create a country full of the smartest, brightest, most inquisitive minds on the planet. The brains you insist on our youth having now will carry us all later, no matter how terrifying or beautiful the future becomes. For almost a century America has held that education is a necessity, but we should be cognizant of increasing the length of that education as our citizen's lifespans increase.

****

22) There is an Alternative to Lawyers Running the Country

For many of us, our careers take more time and energy than anything else in our lives. Our chosen professions speak volumes not only about who we are, but what we believe in. With one's job being so important in one's life, you'd think there would be more insistence on career background diversity for the top leadership roles in the US government.

There isn't.

Forty percent of our highest politicians in the US Congress are l awyers. And it's been like that, or even more stilted, for a long time. Does that seem right?

The legal profession is often criticized in public in a blase way. Some of the criticism is fair, and some of it is nonsense. As a non-attorney political candidate, I'm not here to bash lawyers, some of whom are my close friends and advisors. However, I'm rather convinced one of the largest problems with US politics is that it's overrun with the profession of legal-minded people, who have a bad habit of creating evermore bureaucracy. In fact, I'm wondering if the US has lost its way as of late because too many attorneys are steering the wheel of our nation. I'm betting a system that has more career and education diversity across the government would result in a better nation, a better economy, and better social policies. So what can we do?

Philosophically, I've never been a fan of actions that let a lesser qualified person get better treatment or advantages than a more qualified person, especially in the workplace. The problem, though, is that massive inequalities exist for society at large, and how one becomes "more qualified" is partially tied to one's background and circumstances. That's why to keep society moving forward, helping the lesser qualified person (often the far more underrepresented person, too) is important and sometimes very necessary—especially if as a country we believe in the spirit of democracy.

With this in mind, I see only two realistic ways (and a third default method) to get other non-attorney politicians into office.

The first is to simply put a legal cap on the amount of lawyers (and any other single profession, for that matter—we wouldn't want all bankers running everything either). To keep a fair playing field, maybe we could have a lottery or rotation system deciding how many attorneys can serve in the three branches of US Government and in what states. Of course, such an idea is interesting to contemplate, but it's totally unlikely to happen, as it's somewhat authoritarian.

A second, perhaps more likely way might be to give non-attorney politicians a better advantage at being elected in the first place. For example, generous federal and state funding for campaigns could be made available to qualified non-legal degreed candidates. And many other incentives could be provided to push non-lawyers into office, such as public promotion campaigns that advocate diversified career backgrounds of its US government leaders. I'm thinking STEM advocates would love this.

Of course, there's a default method, too. Some futurists, including myself, see a time coming when lawyers—human lawyers that is— will become obsolete.

The rise of artificial intelligence is poised to affect many jobs, and the legal profession is definitely included. Free online legal advice has already caused law schools to have lower amounts of entrance applications, since less lawyers may be needed in the future. So if we just wait it out for 20 or 30 years, when superintelligent AI arrives, we might not have to worry about attorneys running the country. They won't exist, at least not in human form.

There's a problem with that argument, though. With lawyers mostly in charge of the nation and its laws, it's unlikely they are going to let technology sabotage the legal field and their careers—at least not too much. In the near future, expect attorneys to try to pass stringent regulations on AI development and the robot revolution in the name of national security and stability—but really, in an effort to protect their livelihoods and dominance of US politics.

Either way, with human or computer lawyers, there's simply too much red tape created by the legal profession in politics. When asked earlier this year to comment on the large amount of lawyers entering the 114th US Congress (213 in total of 535 places), Cornell Law School's Josh Chafetz told The National Law Journal, "I suppose my only real thought would be that that's probably too many lawyers—especially when you consider that the president is a lawyer and all of our judges are lawyers. To have a government that is so overwhelmingly dominated by people with a common training risks shutting out other ways of thinking about what our politics could be."

Here's the thing: Being a lawyer is more than a profession—it's a state of mind. To the attorney, everything is settled in court, by a judge, through guiding rules, historical precedence, and subjective presentation of ideas and facts. Lawyering is essentially becoming proficient at abstract thinking, and society must be careful to leave its operations in the hands of people who deal mostly in the abstract.

Doctors, engineers, farmers, plumbers, and just about every other profession don't look at the world in the same way as attorneys do. Doctors have taken an oath to help their patients by administering the best medicines and performing surgical procedures. Engineers must make sure their buildings don't fall on its inhabitants and that the lights work. Farmers must grow food with whatever conditions they're given or people don't eat. Plumbers must make sure sewage pipes flow freely and don't backup. These are not abstract pursuits. They are the nuts and bolts of a material world.

Abstract ideas are easy to get lost in—just think of the fascination with abstract art, which I also enjoy. But it's no way to run a country.

"With almost 1.3 million lawyers—more by far than any other country, and more as a percentage of the national population than almost all others—the United States is choking on litigation, regulation, and disputation," says Jeff Jacoby, a Boston Globe columnist with a law degree. "Everything is grist for the lawyers' mills. Anyone can be sued for anything, no matter how absurd or egregious. And everyone knows how expensive and overwhelming a legal assault can be. The rule of law is essential to a free and orderly society, but too much law and lawyering makes democratic self-rule impossible, and common sense legally precarious."

Imagine for a moment if the US government was run by a cross-section of people, all who have had different careers and varying educations. Imagine if the massive medical profession of America's workforce was represented by surgeons, nurses, and scientists. Imagine if blue-collar workers sat in Congress and debated inequality. What if teachers dealt with education reform? What if designers wondered about infrastructure development of the country and had political power to implement it? What if journalists dealt directly with defense and military policy? What if accountants and mathematicians debated spending budgets? What if scientists dealt with environmental issues and laws?

When I imagine these things, it's not hard to picture a better America—one that more closely reflects the will, image, and dreams of its people. America was made great by the promise of the American Dream: the idea that you can become successful through your hard work. I tend to believe we should consider mandating that non-legal professions be equally involved in government and leadership of our country. A system could be developed where all major professions are approximately represented according to their numbers and societal impact.

Many people seem to be dissatisfied with the plight of American politics and our nation's future. Perhaps if we really want to improve our country, we should start by electing leaders who design and build our homes, who teach science and history to our children, who diagnose and cure our diseases, who plant and grow our foods, and who create new technologies and innovations that improve our lives. We can change America by insisting new types of people lead our government.

****

23) The Second Amendment Isn't Prepared for a 3D Printed Army

Imagine this: A disgruntled citizen borrows $30,000 from his credit cards. With the money he buys a sophisticated 3D printer off eBay and begins secretly printing and building a hundred drones in his garage. Then he downloads internet blueprints of 3D gun printing tech that can be adapted to arm his drones.

The terrorist decides he wants some of his drones outfitted to carry droppable Molotov cocktails and glass containers of hydrochloric acid. He pre-programs some of the drones to shoot or crash into specific targets using over-the-counter navigation software. Other drones the terrorist plans to fly himself.

He decides to target the downtown of a city, or a college campus, or a crowded strip mall, or even a football stadium during a playoff game. He's created a warzone with his drone army.

Welcome to the new world of terrorism. This type of attack hasn't happened yet, but the technology to do it is already here—and getting cheaper and more easily accessible every day.

As a political candidate and US citizen, I want protection from this kind of thing from the US Constitution. Unfortunately, it's not coming—not because the constitution is an unworthy document, but because it was written with quill pens by patriots whose ideas of weapons in 1787 was a musket or a sword. Technology is outpacing the law, and few people are aware at how vulnerable this phenomenon is leaving citizens.

The Second Amendment reads: *A well regulated Militia, being necessary to the security of a free State, the right of the people to keep and bear Arms, shall not be infringed.*

The key word there is "arms."

The landmark 2008 Supreme Court case, District of Columbia v. Heller, which helped define the term "arms," established that an individual has the right to own a firearm for lawful reasons, including self-defense in one's residence.

But this doesn't clear up whether a person can have an on-demand armed drone army in their garage at home. In the near future, that little word "arms" is going to become even more controversial than it has been. Just think of the Iron Man suit, something the military is already developing. Is that a type of weapon, if you wore it and walked into a bank? What about a driverless car transporting dynamite on San Francisco's Golden Gate Bridge? How about a smartphone that puts out physically hurtful sound waves—something that scientists are working on?

The point is, what the founding fathers considered necessary freedoms to protect a free state is changing dramatically—and political confusion is abundant. Tech development—even if Moore's law can't hold up—grows tremendously every year. In 20 years, weapons will likely exist that we haven't even thought of yet. Take, for example, the field of military cybersecurity, which barely was a thing a decade ago and now is a major concern.

So how can a nearly 230-year-old document keep up? Take a deep breath loyal constitutionalists—and repeat after me: It can't. The US Constitution has to be gutted. We need to create a constitution that's malleable and ready to adjust radically every few years to changing times and accelerating technology. And that document must throw nearly all historical precedent out the door.

Look at the coming times we face. There's no historical framework to instruct us for whether we should grant conscious, sapient robots personhood and citizenship. Or whether only the rich have access to genetic editing tech that literally improves children's IQ before they're born. Or whether a Universal Basic Income should be implemented because of mass automization. The US Constitution just can't keep up—and honestly, nor can our three branches of government: Executive, Legislative, and Judicial. There's just too much going on with radical science and tech innovation.

Consider my biohacker friends trying to replace eating and world hunger by splicing photosynthesis capabilities into their bodies. This gives me a chuckle when considering the Constitution, since many of the founding fathers were farmers. What would they think? The end of food? Why not? It would solve a lot of problems.

All these issues add up to why I'm endorsing a newly written *Transhumanist Bill of Rights* that aims to add language to the US Bill of Rights. But my futurist document doesn't help other parts of the US Constitution out much, since the Constitution also tackles ideas way beyond personhood and personal rights—and instead focuses on how a country out to be run.

Back to the terrorist and the $30,000 drone army in his garage. In a quickly changing environment, the safety of citizens and its people rest with sound policy that prepares them for conflict and catastrophe before they happen—or to avoid it entirely. While I believe in the right to bear some arms (and have been to war zones as a journalist where people didn't have guns and were being crushed by occupying forces), some lone person attacking the downtown of a major city with a drone army is too much for me.

The Second Amendment was put in place to protect a free state and its people, and to give individuals that power to do so. Now in a world where it's possible within 25 years a 3D printer will be able to help mostly print a dirty bomb that can take out a whole city, I wonder if the amendment can hold out.

In fact, I'm guessing that entire new wording and interpretations will have to be drawn up to address the issues. It'll certainly have to address that personal drones, robots, and cyberterror are the future of arms, and not guns.

America is changing. It's not because people, their desire for freedom, or their morals are much different than 200+ years ago, but because technology is changing the rules and maybe even the entire game. We better rewrite our policies and laws soon. Maybe we even better start from scratch.

****

24) We Need a New Government Agency and Tort Reform to Conquer all Disease

Scientists increasingly agree that we're fast approaching a moment in medicine—probably within 25 years—where we won't just be significantly lengthening human lifespans, but probably conquering death too.

If this is the case, then the 150,000 people+ who die every day on Earth is doubly tragic. We may soon look back and mourn these hundreds of millions—our parents, friends, and loved ones—who just missed the time in history of achieving indefinite lifespans instead of ending up in a grave.

What this all means is science is nearing the final leg of the greatest race it's ever been in. Medicine's main goal will no longer be to just improve health, but to attempt to guarantee survival for every person that exists on the planet. Unfortunately, one significant challenge to medicine succeeding in this noble life extension aim comes from the most ironic and unlikely of places: the Food and Drug Administration (FDA).

On average, a new drug takes at least 10 years from creation to arrival in your cabinet in America. Additionally, Matthew Herper at *Forbes* reports that about $5 billion is spent on average in developing a new drug. New medical devices—especially life saving ones—take upwards of seven years to hit the market. For patients, some who are dying to get the drugs and devices, this may as well be an eternity. Nearly all of this has to do with the FDA and the bureaucratic labyrinth that exists to make sure medicine is safe in America.

Now don't get me wrong, I also want safe medicine. And for the most part, the FDA does that. But sometimes there are more important things than safe medicine, especially if you're suffering from a debilitating and terminal disease. For example, many people believe access to medicine before they die is more important than whether that medicine is safe or not. And with such a long, laborious, and costly medical approval process in the US, many inventors and companies that would like to create new medicine don't do it because of the prohibitive procedure of bearing a product from conception to sale.

It's no wonder start-up companies are opening shop in Europe and China, where clinical trials costs less and regulations in some cases are more lax. The obvious question is: How long can this continue before another nation becomes the pharmaceutical and medical device global powerhouse?

Imagine if you're a company, and you have a new heart disease drug that you want to create. You'd have to have cash on hand for a decade (or know you could get it) before you might—if the FDA approved you through its multiple stages—to make single sale on a drug. Now imagine you do the same process in Eastern Europe or Asia, and you only need half the cash on hand. You'd have a far better chance at actually bringing a life saving drug to market and making sure you company can survive until it does so.

There are a lot of reasons for the FDA's notorious regulatory hurdles. Rather than blame them specifically, though, it's easier to blame the true culprits—the vampires of capitalism: lawyers. They have made it so that a few deaths from a new drug (even one that helps tens of thousands of people live far better and longer) are enough to make it so that drug makers won't develop or carry the drug. Class action lawsuits are a reputation killer and simply too much a financial burden.

Tort reform, which I strongly support as a political candidate, would have a major impact on the medical development field. But more importantly, we must bear in mind the concept of life hours—the concept that human beings have a certain amount of healthy, productive hours of life in them, and those hours should be protected at all cost. If a drug has made it so that a large section of people benefit and live longer, more productively because of it, then it's okay that a few don't and possibly even die. We must remember the greater good for society and ourselves, and measure life by life hours, and not our feelings.

I understand this type of thinking is not politically correct, but being politically correct is what healthy people have the luxury of doing. Those dying—those having their cells eaten by cancer, or their minds ravished by Alzheimer's, or the blood flow in their arteries stopped by blockage—tend to be more interested in what makes them healthy and what is functional for American medicine.

What's functional, given the amount of red tape the FDA and the legal system has cast all over American medical development in America is one of two choices.

We could attempt a total reboot of the FDA. Fire everyone and rehire those who are worthy. Ditch the old rules. Limit attorneys having anything to do with policy creation. Set new mandates that insist upon preserving people's life hours, not the bandage pharmaceutical culture America has as its main source of medicine. Also, make this new entity not just an institution that monitors and approves new drugs, but have it be an entity that facilitates America to systematically cure every disease on planet Earth—something that is possible to achieve in the next 50 years if enough resources are put into it. And lastly—the final nail in the coffin—change the FDA name to something new. Something bolder.

I support these actions against the FDA in theory. But I know it's not realistic. One doesn't just change such an embedded government institution without massive controversy, Congressional will, and Presidential support. So the other alternative makes more sense: Leave the FDA alone, but create a totally new institution—sanctioned by the government—whose mission is to encourage and green-light the speedy development of experimental drugs and medical devices for the public. Make it law that this new institution's drug and medical device trial period could not be more than a third of the FDA's average. The government sanction for such a new institution would give the needed authority for US citizens to trust (to some extent) the treatments they receive, while always understanding that such medicine was experimental.

The new drug and medical device field could then be split between traditional FDA approved medicine, and medicine that was more experimental and less proven—but cutting edge and, most importantly, available. Companies developing medical products would have the choice of which approval they sought. But both would be available to consumers with prescriptions.

Such a system would stop our innovators and scientists from going overseas, and keep jobs in America. It would also keep America in the running to remain the world leader in medicine as we enter the transhumanist age. Most importantly, it would keep America in the race to save lives without jeopardizing its regard for the public's safety. It transfers the responsibility to consumers, which any government should always strive to do. If consumers didn't want experimental or fast tracked medicines, they simply could go for FDA approved products only.

The reality is that every year millions of super sick and terminally ill people would likely be willing to try experimental drugs and medical devices rather than suffer or die. America should lead the way to help these people by creating a bold new institution that fast tracks these possible remedies and cures. It's the humane thing to do.

****

25) We Must Destroy Nukes Before an Artificial Intelligence Learns to Use Them

On a warm October day, videographer Roen Horn, *Slate* columnist Mark O'Connell, and I visited the White Sands Missile Range, which is home to an outdoor missile museum. Still an active military base, it takes a 10-minute security inspection and a stamped clearance to even be able to enter the area.

I was in the middle of political campaign, and we were after a photo-op of transhumanists in front of missiles. The fact that 25,000 nuclear bombs exist around the world is reason enough to try to warn the public. A detonated bomb in a mega-city could easily kill hundreds of thousands.

Generally speaking, many transhumanists strongly advocate for using science and technology to eliminate death. This means much of the movement and its scientists are focusing on stopping aging through gene therapies, overcoming disease through robotic organs, and living longer via radical diets or imbibing a handful of pills every day.

While I actively support all these longevity techniques, it's important to realize that death doesn't just come through the human aging and disease, but also through human folly. This is why I believe transhumanists should also be deeply concerned about existential risk, such as nuclear warfare. I personally advocate for dismantling all nuclear weapons.

Thankfully, it's not just transhumanists who are concerned about such risks. Plenty of politicians in recent campaigns noted that nuclear threat is a great worry.

To me, it's critical that major politicians continue to be vocal about this ongoing dilemma. As a society, we have become complacent to the fact that so many nuclear arms are still out there. But tensions between Russia and America, as well as those of China and America, are a stark reminder we should not ever get complacent. The ongoing rivalry between India and Pakistan, also nuclear heavyweights, should be considered too.

The first nuclear bomb, called Little Boy, was dropped on Hiroshima, Japan on August 6, 1945. Eighty thousand people immediately perished.

Six years before, the creation of the bomb began with a suggestion by Hungarian physicist Leo Szilard and Albert Einstein to President Franklin D. Roosevelt, which culminated with the Manhattan Project, perhaps the most impressive of any technological effort the United States has ever engaged in.

It's sad to me that one of America's greatest technology efforts is one of war. However, it's not only open war civilization should be worried about; it's thievery or malfunction of nuclear arms, too.

Additionally, a major coming worry about nuclear weaponry is the rise of artificial intelligence and a Terminator scenario unfolding. I'm quite certain the highest long term military priority of America is the development and containment of coming artificial intelligence, because whichever country creates a superintelligent AI first would probably have the ability to break and rewrite all nuclear codes on the planet. Such power could change the global political landscape overnight.

Walking around the missile park—with its big yellow signs warning visitors to beware of rattlesnakes—it's impossible not to get the feeling this is war exhibit dedicated to men and their toys of fighting. An indoor museum is attached to the outdoor missile park, and nearly every portrait of the missile base founders and operators was of a gray-haired Caucasian man steeped in the means of warfare. Looking at those pictures, I longed for a new, diverse generation of humanitarian-minded influencers and leaders to come reinvent how we handle the security of Americans and people on Earth. Clearly, there must be a better way than the ironic amassing of tens-of-thousands of four-story tall killing machines.

****

26) How Brain Implants (and Other Technology) Could Make the Death Penalty Obsolete

The death penalty is one of America's most contentious issues. Critics complain that capital punishment is inhumane, pointing out how some executions have failed to quickly kill criminals (and instead tortured them). Supporters of the death penalty fire back saying capital punishment deters violent crime in society and serves justice to wronged victims. Complicating the matter is that political, ethnic, and religious lines don't easily distinguish death penalty advocates from its critics. In fact, only 31 states even allow capital punishment, so America is largely divided on the issue.

Regardless of the debate—which shows no signs of easing as we head into more major elections—I think technology will change the entire conversation in the next 10 to 20 years, rendering many of the most potent issues obsolete.

For example, it's likely we will have cranial implants in 15 years' time that will be able to send signals to our brains that manipulate our behaviors. Those implants will be able to control out-of-control tempers and violent actions—and maybe even unsavory thoughts. This type of tech raises the obvious question: Instead of killing someone who has committed a terrible crime, should we instead alter their brain and the way it functions to make them a better person?

Recently, the commercially available Thync device made headlines for being able to alter our moods. Additionally, nearly a half million people already have implants in their heads, most to overcome deafness, but some to help with Alzheimer's or epilepsy. So the technology to change behavior and alter the brain isn't science fiction. The science, in some ways, is already here—and certainly poised to grow, especially with Obama's $3 billion dollar BRAIN initiative, of which $70 million went to DARPA, partially for cranial implant research.

Some people may complain that implants are too invasive and extreme. But similar outcomes—especially in altering criminal's minds to better fit society's goals—may be accomplished by genetic engineering, nanotechnology, or even super drugs. In fact, many criminals are already given powerful drugs, which make them quite different that they might be without them. After all, some people—including myself—believe much violent crime is a version of mental disease.

With so much scientific possibility on the near-term horizon of changing someone's criminal behavior and attitudes, the real debate society may end up having soon is not whether to execute people, but whether society should advocate for cerebral reconditioning of criminals—in other words, a lobotomy.

Because I want to believe in the good of human beings, and I also think all human existence has some value, I'm on the lookout for ways to preserve life and maximize its usefulness in society.

One other method that could be considered for death row criminals is cryonics. The movie *Minority Report*, which features precogs who can see crime activity in the future, show other ways violent criminals are dealt with: namely a form of suspended animation where criminals dream out their lives. So the concept isn't unheard of. With this in mind, maybe violent criminals even today should legally be given the option for cryonics, to be returned to a living state in the future where the reconditioning of the brain and new preventative technology—such as ubiquitous surveillance—means they could no longer commit violent acts.

Speaking of extreme surveillance—that rapidly growing field of technology also presents near-term alternatives for criminals on death row that might be considered sufficient punishment. We could permanently track and monitor death row criminals. And we could have an ankle brace (or implant) that releases a powerful tranquilizer if violent behavior is reported or attempted.

Surveillance and tracking of criminals would be expensive to monitor, but perhaps in five to 10 years' time basic computer recognition programs in charge of drones might be able to do the surveillance affordably. In fact, it might be cheapest just to have a robot follow a violent criminal around all the time, another technology that also should be here in less than a decade's time. Violent criminals could, for example, only travel in driverless cars approved and monitored by local police, and they'd always be accompanied by some drone or robot caretaker.

Regardless, in the future, it's going to be hard to do anything wrong anyway without being caught. Satellites, street cameras, drones, and the public with their smartphone cameras (and in 20 years' time their bionic eyes) will capture everything. Simply put, physical crimes will be much harder to commit. And if people knew they were going to be caught, crime would drop noticeably. In fact, I surmise in the future, violent criminals will be caught far more frequently than now, especially if we have some type of trauma alert implant in people—a device that alerts authorities when someone's brain is signaling great trouble or trauma (such as a victim of a mugging).

Inevitably, the future of crime will change because of technology. Therefore, we should also consider changing our views on the death penalty. The rehabilitation of criminals via coming radical technology, as well as my optimism for finding the good in people, has swayed me to gently come out publicly against the death penalty.

Whatever happens, we shouldn't continue to spend billions of dollars of tax payer money to keep so many criminals in jail. The US prison system costs four times the entire public education system in America. To me, this financial fact is one of the greatest ongoing tragedies of American economics and society. We should use science and technology to rehabilitate and make criminals contribute positively to American life—then they may not be criminals anymore, but citizens adding to a brighter future for all of us.

****

27) Could Direct Digital Democracy and a New Branch of Government Improve the US?

Direct Digital Democracy, or DDD, is not new. However, it's a concept that might soon challenge the nature of government around the world.

DDD broadly argues that, with so much technology at people's disposal (70 percent of the world will be using smartphones by 2020), we should be able to influence the actions of our governments and legal systems by being able to universally vote on issues as they occur.

New software programs, and our constant interconnectedness via phones, computers, tablets, and even smartwatches, allow us the ability to form a quick and powerful national opinion—and let government and our leaders know about it in real time.

A major issue with democracy right now is the lag time between when the people express their wishes and when politicians act. Currently, the best we can do is vote in a politician and hope over their term they actually try to keep the promises they made. This system—which most Western countries have—is called representative democracy. The problem, of course, is many politicians don't keep their promises once they've started their jobs. This is especially troubling in the case of US Senators, who serve six years, and are sometimes known to be totally out of touch with their constituents.

DDD brings back power to the people. Over the last 25 years, since use of the internet became commonplace, various public figures have advocated for DDD. Most famously was Ross Perot, who envisioned electronic town hall meetings and campaigned for DDD in his 1992 and 1996 presidential campaigns (Perot preferred to refer to it as "electronic democracy" instead of DDD).

Direct digital democracy is so appealing to the people that I'm wondering if America should formally introduce a fourth branch of federal government that would be entirely based on the concept. Such a DDD branch of government would further balance the powers that be. Currently in the US, the executive (President), judicial (Supreme Court), and legislative (US Congress) branches of the federal government are set up to constantly keep each other from overstepping boundaries and doing stupid things—creating what we know as the checks and balances system.

For over two centuries, this system has mostly worked. But make no mistake, it's a flawed democratic system that doesn't actually do the will of the people, except for at the very moment it elects its representatives. What we could try in America is a fourth branch that actually voices in real time what the people believe.

One benefit of such a system is that it might thwart lobbyists, special interest groups, and backroom government dealings by keeping politicians far more honest. Reports show that only one in five Americans trust their government. DDD would give people an opportunity to show agreement or disagreement with their politicians, including the possibility to vote for impeachment of underperformers.

I think in the future, this fourth branch of government might be something very serious to consider for adherents of democracy. But how would DDD formally work?

Frankly, it could operate in a number of ways, but it probably wouldn't be much different than a simple polling and voting platform that operates on gadgets people own. Many programs offer similar ideas to this already, including Twitter now with its polling abilities. I'm imagining an encrypted Social Security number-based system. Once a month, people all around the country have a chance to voice their opinion in standardized votes on pre-chosen agendas. Americans could tackle the issues the other branches of government are considering, or even issues that are still on the back burners— like whether marijuana should be nationally legalized, or whether we should allow lethal drones in our skies, or whether we should reduce the number of our nearly 7,500 nuclear weapons. In urgent matters, like directly after 9/11, emergency votes could be undertaken.

Because DDD votes would need to have some legal authority to impact the federal checks and balances system we have now in the US government, the US Congress might have to add an amendment to the US Constitution. Of course, the language establishing DDD would have to be such that it creates a legal mandate of action to be followed: This might include certain vetoing powers over other branches of government, as well as the ability to break ties (for example, the Supreme Court just recently had a tie regarding unions). Maybe the DDD vote even should have a say in who gets nominated for the Supreme Court.

A possible problem with DDD might be that not enough people vote on certain issues. In this case, qualifiers could be established that mandate a minimum of 50 percent (or even two-thirds) of the eligible voting population votes.

Elected officials—many who are self-interested lawyers—will surely have other problems with DDD. Mostly, they'll probably complain that America's proposed laws and mandates are highly complex—and each issue comes with hundreds of pages of reading material. While that may be true, I disagree that voters shouldn't tackle them. I think—whether people are informed correctly, partially, or maybe even not at all—they should still have a voice that counts. That's what a checks and balances system in a democracy is all about. Besides, obviously President George W. Bush wasn't correctly informed about weapons of mass destruction when he took America to war in Iraq, so it's not only government officials that are sometimes wrong.

On the flip side, one of the reasons I think many people will like DDD is it gives millennials and youth a much louder voice. Currently in the US, there are nearly 80 million people under the age of 35. Yet, getting them to vote can be difficult for a number of reasons—which often boils down to apathy or schedule conflicts. But quick votes from their smartphones could change that entire issue. America's youth would have a louder voice than it's ever had—and in these changing transhuman times, that could be very helpful.

In the future, technology and the internet will continue to bring us all closer to each other and give us more visibility into our government. We should be open to considering new ways to improve our society and nations using innovative solutions. Democracy and the will of the people is the cornerstone of our modern way of life, but it can always be improved upon to maximize freedom and equality. Direct digital democracy is a fine idea to consider to start in that direction.

****

28) Could an Implant have Saved the Life of the Toddler Attacked by a Disney World Alligator?

Among other tragedies in Florida recently gripping America's attention, a 2-year-old boy was snatched away from its parents by an alligator at Walt Disney World on Wednesday. I have a similar-aged toddler myself, and I followed this heartbreaking story closely. Unfortunately, it ended as horribly as it began, with the recovery of a dead child.

As a tech-minded political candidate, much of my work is based on advocating for radical science and technology to make the world a better place for humans. As a result, I have been advocating for using chip implants in people to help keep them safer. Chip implants are often just the size of a grain of rice and can be injected by a needle in a nearly pain-free 60-second procedure. The implants can do a multiple array of things depending on the type. And much of the technology has been used in pets for over a decade, so it's already been shown to be relatively safe.

I have a RFID NFC chip in my hand that is programmed to send a text saying "Win in 2016" to people who have the right type of phone. To get the text, all you have to do is put your phone by my hand. My chip can also start a car with the right software, hand out a business card electronically, or give out my medical information.

But the future of implants—as well as other wearable tech—may end up being most useful for the safety it provides.

While scene reports claim the father got into the water to save his son, perhaps if that 2-year-old at Disney World had been GPS chipped (or tattooed with a graph chip), the parents could have tracked him on their smartphones. And security might have been able to quickly identify his location in the water, perhaps even fast enough to have rescued him. *The New York Times* reports that the body was tragically found underwater only 10-15 feet from where it was last seen.

That's of little consolation now, of course, and I don't mean to be insensitive to the family's loss, but I do think this tragedy illustrates how implants could help improve public safety. They could help track our children, and adults for that matter, in the case of kidnapping and Amber alerts, or even just when they get lost on a hike in the woods.

An article I wrote at the *Huff Post* discusses the use of a brain implant that goes one step further than GPS tracking by notifying emergency crews of extreme trauma:

Cranial implants and brain wave technology have come a long way in the last few years. Already, hundreds of thousands of people in the world have microchip implants in their heads, consisting of everything from chips to help Parkinson's sufferers to cochlear implants for the deaf to devices to assist Alzheimer's patients with memory loss. For each, this technology allows a better life. DARPA recently announced a $70 million dollar five-year plan to develop implants that can monitor soldier's mental health. It's part of President Obama's new multi-billion dollar BRAIN Initiative.

Implants using Electroencephalography (EEG) technology can read and decipher brain waves. Trauma, however experienced, is a measurable biological phenomenon that can be monitored and captured by an implant device. Scientists must do nothing more than create a trackable chip that sends an emergency signal to nearby authorities when it registers extreme trauma. Help can then arrive quickly to the victim.

Much of the technology for such a device basically already exists. And such a device could be useful for far more than rape or criminal violence, too. Drowning, being burned in a fire, automobile accidents, building collapses, snake bites, kidnappings, bullet

wounds, senior citizens who've fallen down stairs and can't get up—
the list of terrible things that happen to humans goes on and on. The
result of every one of them is almost always the same: brain waves
that manifest extreme trauma—the human's most basic response
and alert system. Regardless what misfortune happens to a human
being, most experts agree that getting victims rapid emergency
assistance is the single best way to help them.

As the father of a 5-year-old who will be attending school next year,
I'm a big believer in the future that all children will get chipped,
perhaps like all children get vaccines in the U.S. It's crazy to me that
we don't develop and use it, especially with our children. I'm looking
into getting my children chipped after this alligator incident and
because, as a controversial political candidate, I have security
issues myself to worry about.

Of course, it's not only implants. It's chip tattoos, graphs, iris scans,
facial recognition, and more. It's also GPS bracelets, rings, wearable
tech T-shirts, or even shoes with tracking tech built into them.
Interestingly, a small industry already exists around children using
tech to keep their whereabouts safe, but they're mostly children with
disabilities—some who have a propensity to wander off.

Perhaps the most advanced case of chipping people has to do with
the military. Reports describe special forces experimenting with them
so they can be tracked. In 2014, for example, the U.S. Department
of Defense announced a $26 million grant for a brain implant that
would record, analyze, and potentially alter live electrical signals to
those struggling with mental illnesses like post-traumatic stress
disorder. The military is getting so interested in implants that I was
recently asked to consult the U.S. Navy on research of chipping their
service people.

All things considered, the trauma alert implant (or even just a basic
GPS tracking one that goes in your hand) sounds like a sensible and
impressive thing. So why don't we have them yet, when we easily
have the tech to create them?

Unfortunately, Americans are skeptical of electronic devices in their
bodies. They've been led to believe they either cause cancer or
they'll malfunction and cause tissue damage. But the truth is tens of
thousands of people have synthetic electronic parts in their bodies.

These include pacemakers and robotic heart valves, like what former Vice President Dick Cheney has. Additionally, a few hundred thousand people already have cochlear implants, which allow deaf people to hear sounds. Most of these devices pose little if any danger and end up dramatically improving health.

And this trend of technology being part of our bodies is only going to increase, since bionic parts are ultimately more durable than biological ones. I estimate that within a decade's time, most people have at least a few synthetic parts merged with their body, whether it's dentures, artificial hips, implants, or even robotic hearts.

Of course the no. 1 complaint about implants in our bodies is the concern of privacy and unwanted surveillance. However, just about everyone already sleeps with a cellphone by their head or keeps one in their pocket, so there's little difference between a small implant and a phone permanently on one's person. In fact, the phone with all its apps has a much higher probability of being tracked. Beyond that is the fact that almost anywhere you go in the modern world, there are cameras. Overcoming surveillance is something I think we all gave up a while back when we allowed tech and the internet to dominate our lives. Just consider a report out in the U.K. that says that there may be as many as 4.2 million cameras in the country. Chicago has over 10,000. We may need to face the facts: We already live in a surveillance society.

The good news is, we'll always have the option to turn an embedded chip implant off, just like we can turn our phones off. So the control will ultimately rest with us.

But perhaps the largest reason some people are wary of implants is religion. In America, 75 percent of the population believes in some form of the Bible, and *Revelations* talks about the Mark of the Beast. When I was on my campaign bus tour and pointed out at rallies that I had an implant, I could literally feel the energy in the air change if people were religious. Bible-believing people looked at me differently, like the implant was a tool of Satan.

The reality is that when the U.S. government issued social security numbers decades ago, religious people said the numbers were the Mark of the Beast too. Frankly, as a secularist, I think religious people should give such apocalyptic stuff a rest and be thankful the transhumanist age will improve humanity's overall well-being. The future of healthcare involves us becoming more cyborg-like, and that will ultimately lead to better health for everyone. When it comes to our loves ones, ensuring their optimum health is the highest priority—and is also quite in line with religious doctrine, too.

There are a lot of reasons to advocate for supporting implants. And it's the reason I believe chipping is going to catch on in a major way in the next few years. It's just too bad it hasn't yet, and as a result, humans are not a prepared to deal with some of the tragedies that occur.

Hopefully in the future, though, technology will break through and make all our lives much safer.

****

29) Reparations: I Became a Pot Felon at 18. I'm Owed More Than an Apology

When asked why I advocate for legalization of recreational drugs, I give a simple answer: Because the government doesn't know what's best for me or others. But there's another reason, and it's far more personal. Twenty-five years ago, as a college freshman, I was arrested by undercover cops for selling $80 worth of marijuana to fellow students. I was convicted of two felonies: distribution and possession of a narcotic. I spent a month in jail.

Long after the ordeal, I feel resentment at the United States government and the old conservative guard who still mostly run it. It's important to understand that becoming a felon, even for a minor non-violent crime, is no small issue when you're 18 years old. In addition to the government taking away your voting and gun rights, and forcing you to submit to random drug tests, a felony makes it extremely difficult to ever get a normal job. A criminal rap is a serious and derogatory social badge.

You'd think there would be some consolation that since my run-in with the law in 1992, America has been slowly withdrawing from its conservative anti-drug fervor. Currently, 28 states allow medical marijuana use, and eight states now have made recreational use legal. Eventually, pot will likely become legal everywhere, including $80 amounts to students on college campuses.

So all is well, right? Wrong.

Millions of other minor drug offenders like me are left holding the bag. It wasn't just the defamatory criminal sentence many of us received. The government confiscated my Jeep Comanche and my beloved Honda motorcycle during the ordeal. What little money I had I spent on lawyers and judicial filings in our convoluted court system. My total financial loss a quarter of a century ago was $20,000 dollars. Had I been able to invest that money in the stock market, for example, I'd have over $100,000 now.

The American Civil Liberties Union reports that 8.2 million people in America were arrested between 2001 and 2010 for marijuana offenses. *The Washington Post* says at least 137,000 people sit in US jails on any given day of the week for weed.

Now that the country is on its glacial way to likely legalizing marijuana and taxing the sale of it like it does beer, where is the official apology, to me and all those others? For many of us, an apology—and the government's inevitable mea culpa when they likely make pot legal across the land—won't be enough.

Some of us also want compensation for the financial damage forced upon us—for the literal theft of our property. Maybe that means a class action lawsuit insisting on government reparation for all damage caused, maybe in the form of tax credits or proceeds from the sale of unused Federal land, so as not to abuse the American taxpayer further over the drug war. It's safe to say—given the damage caused and the lives affected—such a suit would likely be in the billions of dollars.

Whatever happens, don't expect minor drug offenders to forget the harm Uncle Sam has caused now that smoking a joint is finally becoming legal and acceptable.

****

30) Should People Who Pay Zero Federal Income Taxes be Allowed to Vote in Federal Elections?

In 2018, only 44 percent of Americans paid any federal income tax. Of 327 million Americans, about 75 million are under the age of 18. That leaves 252 million Americans, and 44 percent of that is 112 million people.

Think about that for a moment. 112 million Americans didn't pay federal income taxes at all last year. To give that perspective, 2016 saw 137 million Americans vote in Federal US elections. It doesn't take a rocket scientist to see how unfair this is that a giant swath of society that doesn't contribute to America's financial bottom line can also vote for who controls that bottom line.

Let's add a third statistic in the mix. 48 percent of Americans get some sort of government support—everything from food stamps to social security to healthcare.

In my professional life, I'm currently focusing on political issue that few people seem to be discussing: Sometime in the next couple years, China's economy and net worth may surpass that of America. Within a decade, India will likely surpass the US too.

Born 46 years ago in California, I have enjoyed the peace and prosperity America has brought to the world as the globe's undeniable superpower and cultural leader. My parents, who illegally escaped Communist Hungary and came to America after World War II, have also enjoyed America—and the American dream. Like millions of others, they came to states with nothing, found work, and prospered in the middle class.

Over the years, my parents and I have valued our ability to vote. We feel we earned it after paying thousands of dollars in federal taxes most every year for decades. But what of the 112 million Americans who don't pay taxes? The US constitution says they have a right to vote, but is it moral to do so?

I live near San Francisco, where there is a plethora of feces and needles in the streets from the tens of thousands of homeless and drug users. I'm both ashamed and afraid because of safety issues to take my young daughters to visit City Hall. I have to wonder if I want the homeless and drug users voting for how to take care of San Francisco. It seems obvious they'd vote for policy that takes resources from those with means and gives to those without means—which is just what so many Democrat presidential candidates are proposing. Elizabeth Warren wants to forgive all school debt. Bernie Sanders wants free housing for anyone who can't afford it. Joe Biden wants free healthcare for all.

Given these facts, some people are proposing this idea: If you haven't paid any federal income tax for three years, unless you're a full-time student, part of the military, a full-time employed nonprofit worker, or senior citizen on social security, you shouldn't be able to vote in federal elections. Basically, if you're not contributing at the most basic and essential monetary level in America or doing working directly for America's best interest, you shouldn't be deciding policy—which is exactly what voting is.

As controversial as this idea is, there are some longtime supporters of it. The supporters often begin their defense of the idea by pointing out that America is not a democracy anyway—that it's a constitutional republic where landowners were the ones supposed to vote. They have a point, but frankly, I don't care about America's oligarch-like past or using history to justify this position. What I care about is what's fair, what is competitive, and what is functional—and not having voting end up just another form of affirmative action.

Think about it in terms of a business: If you run a company, you don't let non-patrons or non-employees make decisions on how to run that business, because it doesn't take long before that business is unable to carry the weight of advice givers without skin in the game. Inevitably that company will be forced into bankruptcy due to lack of competitiveness and entitlement costs by those who have nothing to lose—and also those who constantly vote to benefit more from the company's resources.

In America's case, we're not going bankrupt yet (though our national debt is skyrocketing to fiscally dangerous limits). But we're about to lose our dominance in the world to the hardworking Chinse and their authoritarian Chinese government—one that doesn't respect many of our cherished freedoms. In this sense, lingering quasi-Communism may still end up defeating Democracy, because China's fine-tuned socialism and steadfast work ethic has been perfected over many decades to succeed. Perhaps it's time that America tries to perfect its so-called democratic constitutional republic, before the world disappears under socialism-fueled tyranny.

Naysayers will say this idea of only federal taxpayers being able to vote in federal elections is a form of tyranny in itself. But plenty of states already have laws that prohibit voting, including for those who are felons, children, severely mentally disabled, or don't have proper identification to prove who they are. I generally think felons should be able to vote, if they pay taxes—and some do because of investments they made.

Critics will also say this idea would mean the very poor would never vote again, since they often don't pay any federal income taxes. For supporters of this idea, that's basically the point. They don't believe the very poor should be voting, because they vote for policies and programs that taxpayers have to pay for, yet infrequently use themselves, if at all. However, it must be noted that paying taxes might then prove a major incentive for the very poor to get jobs to be able to vote.

Critics also say everybody pays many other taxes (property taxes, Capital Gains taxes, payroll taxes, etc.) beyond federal income taxes that reach the bottom line of the federal government of America. This is true, but for this Americans get freeways, military, the FBI, national forest fire services, and a myriad of other benefits including social security and welfare. This idea is only talking about taking away the right to vote for federal offices if you don't pay federal income taxes.

Ultimately, it's not that supporters of this idea don't support democracy, it's that even a right to democracy must be earned—especially when the country operating on democracy is being run by taxpayer money. It's astonishing to me that there are many millions of Americans out there living completely off the government, with little or no intention to contribute in any meaningful monetary way to the success of the United States and its governing bodies.

Of course, it's possible we could get rid of federal income tax altogether and just create a national sales tax on everything to make up tax revenue to run the government. This way everyone would pay their fair share and still get to vote. This and plenty of other alternative ideas to fund the government are worthwhile exploring. But US bureaucracy being what it is, I'm currently trying to explore ways to improve the system we now have in place, which relies heavily on federal income taxes and people paying them.

Today in America, if people want a seat at the table for federal elections, it's morally appropriate they should buy it. And that means actually paying federal income taxes, even if it's just a negligible amount like a yearly $1000 dollars (maybe even less) because that's all they made and can afford. If we don't get clear about our priorities soon, America is going to lose its global leadership role to tyrannical nations. If we're not careful, it'll only be a matter of time then when our voting—regardless who or who isn't allowed to vote—won't make any difference at all.

****

CHAPTER IV: PAST POLITICAL CAMPAIGNS

31) Forget Trump, Zoltan Istvan Wants to be the 'Anti-Death' President

It was maddening. After departing San Francisco in September 2015 and crossing America on my campaign bus to post a Transhumanist Bill of Rights to the US Capitol, the single-page document wouldn't stick to the sandstone wall. Standing on the steps near Capitol Hill's main entrance, I began ripping off more masking tape to try to help my document adhere better. Then I heard the footsteps and yelling behind me. Posting anything on the US Capitol is illegal. Within seconds, police and soldiers carrying M-16s had me surrounded, ordering me to back away.

I turned to everyone and explained what transhumanism was: a social movement that wants to use science and technology to radically change the human species. I told them why posting the *Transhumanist Bill of* Rights was so important: it defended the right of humans to experiment with technology on their bodies; it gave personhood to future sapient individuals such as AI; and it established the core transhumanist aim that people have a universal right to live indefinitely through science.

A guard clutching his machine gun less than a meter away warned me I was going to be arrested. I pondered this, but turned back to the building and re-posted the document on it. The thing was, this wasn't just any document. Nor was transhumanism just any movement. Both were inescapably bound to the future of humankind. And this small act of civil disobedience was just the first step of a long journey - one of radical evolution that would involve human beings uploading their minds into machines, replacing their hearts with bionic ones and using CRISPR genome-editing tech to grow gills so they could breathe underwater. The guard looked at me as if I was insane.

In March 2013, I published a novel called *The Transhumanist Wager*. The book asks a simple question: how far would you go to fight an anti-science world in order to live indefinitely through transhumanism? Protagonist Jethro Knights would start a world war

- and does so in the book. It can be seen as a political manifesto, and although I don't believe in all of the book's Nietzschean philosophy, 18 months after publishing it I announced that I was running for the US presidency. I really do want to create a science-minded world, and I think humanity's well-being and happiness would be better off for it.

Will AI solve all the world's problems when it arrives? Will sex disappear as we install microchips in our brains that stimulate pleasure zones? Will we double our children's IQ with gene-editing techniques and nanotechnology? The questions are endless, the ethics murky. Nonetheless, companies - many of which are where I live in San Francisco - are already working on all these ideas.

My goal with my transhumanist evangelism and the political Transhumanist Party I lead is to spread awareness of the questions, and - on occasion - attempt qualified answers. It's tough going, to say the least. Transhumanist activism is a new concept, and even my *Transhumanist Bill of Rights* won't stick to a slick historic wall.

While I never expected to win the US elections in 2016, I saw my campaign as a way to share transhumanism with the world and to help launch a crucial aspect of futurism that was missing: transhumanist activism. With two years of campaigning behind me, it's been a success, with many milestones reached.

The formation of the US Transhumanist Party in October 2014 helped launch a dozen other transhumanist initiatives around the world - including the creation of futurist parties with their own candidates. There are now a handful of transhumanist politicians running for office around the world.

Another major milestone was the Immortality Bus tour which ended in December 2015 in Washington DC. In a vehicle shaped like a huge coffin as a symbol against death, my team and I spent four months crossing America spreading the transhumanism gospel. Media attention was intense, and we held rallies, staged street protests, and met the public on transhumanist issues.

In November 2015, we drove the bus uninvited to the 32,000-person strong Church of the Highlands in Alabama. The first 30 minutes went well. My team, two journalists and I wandered around the huge campus and were even given a tour by a pastor. Then the congregation members began Googling transhumanism. Within minutes the campus was put on lockdown. Gun-toting church members escorted us off the property.

Transhumanism will lead humanity forward to understand what seems like a simple truth: that the specter of aging and death are unwanted, and we should strive to control and eliminate them.

Today, the idea of conquering death with science is still seen as strange. So is the idea of merging with machines - one of transhumanists' most important long-term goals. But once bionic eyes are better than human eyes - something that will likely happen within the next decade or so - the elective upgrades will start. So will using robots for household chores and getting chip implants (I have one in my hand). So will CRISPR genetic editing create a new age of curing of disease and enhancing our physical form.

Embracing transhumanism will become normal, and we will become a civilization that seeks to upgrade our bodies and lives much like we currently upgrade our smartphones.

****

32) Why a Presidential Candidate is Driving a Giant Coffin Called the Immortality Bus Across America

Since the beginning of recording history, it's always been assumed humans could not escape death and the grave. Yet in the 21st Century, millions of people around the planet are coming to the startling revelation that modern science and technology may soon be able to overcome human mortality. This has not escaped the media, which is increasingly reporting on this phenomenon.

Radical longevity science is sound. Recent studies in mice have shown aging is something that can be slowed down, stopped, and most likely even reversed. Longevity activists and transhumanists — those that want to use science and technology to radically improve the human being — are very excited about this and hope to have the choice to live indefinitely in the near future. In fact, as the Transhumanist Party's 2016 US Presidential candidate, I'm basing much of my campaign on spreading the word that aging should be treated like a disease — and not destiny. And I hope to effectively spread this message by driving a 40-foot bus that looks like a giant coffin across America — a stark reminder that aging and death affects us all unless we do something about it.

On my tour called the "Immortality Bus," I'm hoping to share with others that we should support a society and culture that is strongly pro-science and pro-longevity. My team and I plan to have embedded journalists aboard the bus, documenting our trip and enlivening the conversation.

Unfortunately, many people in America and around the world — especially those who believe in afterlives — are neutral or even oppose stopping biological death and aging with science. They feel it challenges what is natural in the human species. Transhumanists call these people "deathists," those who believe and accept that death is a desirable fate.

Complicating matters for transhumanists is the fact that the 535-person U.S. Congress, the current U.S. President, and all members of the U.S. Supreme Court are 100 percent religious and believe in afterlives. Ultimately, this means the American government has little policy incentive to stop death or to put national resources behind life extension science to make citizen's lives far longer and healthier. As a result, nearly 7,500 Americans die every day (about 150,000 die daily worldwide), even though the science is literally out there to stop it. Longevity scientists and transhumanists believe this is an incalculable tragedy.

Reuters reports that renowned gerontologist Dr. Aubrey de Grey, chief scientist at SENS Research Foundation and the Anti-aging Advisor at the U.S. Transhumanist Party, thinks scientists will be able to control aging in the near future, "I'd say we have a 50/50 chance of bringing aging under what I'd call a decisive level of medical control within the next 25 years or so."

It's not just scientists who are advocating for much longer lives. A plethora of life extension and transhumanist activity has been occurring around the world recently. Google's company Calico was recently formed to fight aging. So was startup Human Longevity, a $70 million dollar company founded by longevity entrepreneur J. Craig Venter, X Prize founder Peter Diamandis, and Dr. Robert Hariri. Even billionaires like Oracle's Larry Ellison and Peter Thiel are putting money into trying to live indefinitely.

I'm hoping my Immortality Bus will become an important symbol in the growing longevity movement around the world. It will be my way of challenging the public's apathetic stance on whether dying is good or not. By engaging people with a provocative, drivable giant coffin, debate is sure to occur across the United States and hopefully around the world. I'm a firm believer that the next great civil rights debate will be on transhumanism: Should we use science and technology to overcome death and become a far stronger species?

The Immortality Bus will begin rolling down American highways in early September stopping at rallies and events, instigating the kind of conversation America and the world needs to challenge outdated cultural ideals—many which are holding science, technology, and medicine back. Robotic hearts, stem cell technology, designer babies, 3D printed organs, and gene therapy are all controversial, but we should pursue them nonetheless because they represent a chance at improved health for the species.

The biggest concern I expect to address on my bus tour is about overpopulation. It's a valid concern. However, I'm not overly worried about life extension science making the world more crowded. Many people assume just because humans stop dying, the planet will become way more overpopulated. But this is not necessarily the case. What many people don't consider is that technology — according to recent reports at the World Bank — has been raising the standard of living for the entire species over the last 30 years, and will continue to do so. As a rule, the higher the standard of living around the world, the less children people have. In fact, if people knew there were going to live far longer than a standard 75-year lifespan — let's say maybe 500 years — many probably wouldn't have children at all for the first few hundred years. Additionally, new green technologies on the horizon will allow us to better distribute the Earth's precious resources to make this planet more ecologically pristine again.

Science is on the cusp of achieving something monumental for human beings — the possibility of overcoming death. The Immortality Bus is a striking symbol aimed at bringing the conversation of life extension science into the mainstream. Like the great bus tours of the 1960's that brought a culture of hippie love to America and the West, the Immortality Bus hopes to bring a culture of desiring far longer lifespans via science.

Perhaps the most important stop on my Immortality Bus tour will be at the U.S. Capitol building, where my team and I plan to deliver a *Transhumanist Bill of Rights* to the US Congress. The bill will advocate for government policy to support indefinite lifespans in our species, as well as the use of synthetic and robotic technology to live healthier and better.

The Immortality Bus is a humanitarian mission. In fact, it's a transhumanitarian mission. We believe in the 21st century everybody has a universal right to a happy and indefinite lifespan, regardless of their heritage, age, or income. Our goal is not only to make your life and the lives of your loved ones better, but to do this for all the people on Earth.

****

33) Zoltan Istvan: Immortality Bus Delivers *Transhumanist Bill of Rights* to US Capitol

After months of traveling across the country on a national bus tour, the coffin-shaped Immortality Bus drove into Washington DC and successfully delivered a newly created *Transhumanist Bill of Rights* to the US Capitol. The delivery of the futurist-themed bill—which aims to push into law cyborg and anti-aging civil rights—ends a national tour for the bus that began its journey in San Francisco on September 5th, 2015.

Crowdfunded on Indiegogo, the provocative Immortality Bus has caught the attention of both America and the world. Highlighted in major media ranging from a 10,000+ word feature in *The Verge* to a CraveCast podcast on *CNET* to a leading front page story on

BBC.com, the Immortality Bus has been making waves with its controversial message: Science and technology can overcome human death—and will likely do so in the next 25 years.

Much of my US Presidential campaign for the Transhumanist Party—which used the bus as a vehicle to spread a techno-optimistic message—also reiterates this same immortality agenda. I believe if the US Government would dedicate $1 trillion dollars to life extension, longevity, and anti-aging industries, we could likely soon conquer death as a species. For some a trillion dollars may seem like a lot of money, but consider that the US government will spend approximately $6 trillion dollars all together on the Iraq War. Surely, overcoming death through modern medicine and science for all Americans seems a much better idea that fighting far-off wars in places most of us will never visit.

With this in mind, the *Transhumanist Bill of Rights* seeks to declare that all Americans (and people of all nationalities, as well) in the 21st Century deserve a "universal right" to live indefinitely and eliminate involuntary suffering through science and technology. Those ideas are conveyed in Articles 1, 2 and 6 of the one-page bill. Specifically, Article 6 establishes that we should seek to treat "aging as a disease," something a number of leading gerontologists also endorse.

I penned the *Transhumanist Bill of Rights* on the steps of the US Supreme Court in November 2015. Once the document was completed, the following day I read out loud the document at the steps of the US Capitol, then posted it to the building (it didn't stick well), and then also hand delivered it to Senator Barbara Boxer's office (my California representative)—covers a number of essential futurist civil rights topics. The bill mandates we protect our species and the planet from existential risk (including environmental destruction, rogue artificial intelligence, and the 25,000 nuclear weapons that currently exist). The bill also calls for renewed commitment to space travel, as well as a government's promise to not put cultural, ethnic, or religious policies before the general health and longevity of its citizens.

Finally, the bill emphasizes the right to morphological freedom: the right to do with one's body whatever one wants so long as it doesn't hurt another person. This is especially important in the gene editing /

designer baby age, which has recently been the cause of much discussion in the scientific community. Unfortunately, some of this talk has been disturbingly anti-progress with calls for a moratorium on such technology. I strongly disagree with scientific moratoriums—unless they are directly and obviously harming people today—which is one reason why we need a bill of rights to protect the interests of human health, evolution, and progress.

Below is a copy of the original *Transhumanist Bill of Rights*. While the bill has been carefully considered by myself and other transhumanists, and we hope it will be incorporated someway into law by the United States of America and other governments, the bill is not static and may evolve further as science and technologies evolve. Futurists generally believe no bill of rights, declaration, or constitution should ever remain permanent and unbendable in the transhumanist age—an age where science and technology are dramatically and rapidly changing our lives and our experience of the universe. (Version 3.0 of the bill has recently been crowdsourced and published in 2019, and Version 2.0 was published by *Wired* in *2018*).

TRANSHUMANIST BILL OF RIGHTS (original version)

Preamble: Whereas science and technology are now radically changing human beings and may also create future forms of advanced sapient and sentient life, transhumanists establish this TRANSHUMANIST BILL OF RIGHTS to help guide and enact sensible policies in the pursuit of life, liberty, security of person, and happiness.

Article 1. Human beings, sentient artificial intelligences, cyborgs, and other advanced sapient life forms are entitled to universal rights of ending involuntary suffering, making personhood improvements, and achieving an indefinite lifespan via science and technology.

Article 2. Under penalty of law, no cultural, ethnic, or religious perspectives influencing government policy can impede life extension science, the health of the public, or the possible maximum amount of life hours citizens possess.

Article 3. Human beings, sentient artificial intelligences, cyborgs, and other advanced sapient life forms agree to uphold morphological freedom—the right to do with one's physical attributes or intelligence (dead, alive, conscious, or unconscious) whatever one wants so long as it doesn't hurt anyone else.

Article 4. Human beings, sentient artificial intelligences, cyborgs, and other advanced sapient life forms will take every reasonable precaution to prevent existential risk, including those of rogue artificial intelligence, asteroids, plagues, weapons of mass destruction, bioterrorism, war, and global warming, among others.

Article 5. All nations and their governments will take all reasonable measures to embrace and fund space travel, not only for the spirit of adventure and to gain knowledge by exploring the universe, but as an ultimate safeguard to its citizens and transhumanity should planet Earth become uninhabitable or be destroyed.

Article 6. Involuntary aging shall be classified as a disease. All nations and their governments will actively seek to dramatically extend the lives and improve the health of its citizens by offering them scientific and medical technologies to overcome involuntary aging.

****

34) What I Learned Running for President and Election Changes that Should be Made

Last week, I was included on ISideWith.com, a site that matches users with presidential candidates after answering a 5-minute political questionnaire. Traffic to my campaign soared, since the site boasts 43 million users. There are nearly 1900 FEC registered 2016 US presidential candidates, but only eight of us still running have matching profiles on ISideWith.

It highlights a truth about US politics—that running for president is broadly a contest of media. And if anyone doubts this, the case in point is Donald Trump. If you can regularly and prominently get into the major media, you can be a contender for president. If you can't, then no one knows who you are—even if you have the best ideas or experience out there.

In October 2014, when I formed the science and tech-focused Transhumanist Party and began my run as a presidential candidate, I was quite naïve. I imagined I'd waltz into the American political scene, get my name on a bunch of state ballots, and make a legitimate run for the White House. I never expected to win, but I believed I could challenge and possibly change a widely criticized political system.

I was wrong. The system is nearly impenetrable, bound by rules designed decades and even centuries ago. Those rules are specifically made to keep radicals like me out—even if the two major party candidates are markedly disliked, as they are this cycle. For starters, it takes many millions of dollars to get on crucial state ballots, like my home state of California, where I am neither on the ballot or even a write-in. Those millions of dollars must pay for an army of staffers who peddle door to door to gain the approximately 880,000 signatures needed for an independent to gain ballot access to all 50 states. And getting signatures supporting an unorthodox transhumanist candidate like myself is even more difficult. It can range from $3 to $10 a signature.

To make this crystal clear, let's consider the case of the Libertarian Party, the third largest political party in America. For the first time since 1996, the party's candidate, former New Mexico Governor Gary Johnson (a friend of mine), will be on the ballot in all 50 states. Twenty years is a long time for Libertarians to wait to finally be on all the ballots again. It won't matter much though in terms of votes, since the Clinton and Trump campaigns have received at least as much as 25 times the amount in campaign contributions as Johnson—and I've learned that running for president is largely a matter of resources, not leadership or even charisma.

With such overwhelming odds against my candidacy and tiny political party from the start, I chose to bypass the battle to get on state ballots and instead focus using media to move the transhumanism movement ahead. After all, only very rarely have third parties in America affected the outcome of the elections anyway. Like it or not, you are stuck with an elephant or a donkey-headed leader.

The good news, though, is the internet is making a run for the presidency a good way to get attention for a cause like transhumanism. It may only take five minutes to file a candidacy form with the FEC to run for US president, but the legitimacy in many people's minds is real. Some candidates out there are using this for real good for the country, like the Nutrition Party and its candidate Rod Silva, which is trying to improve the way America eats. Or the Marijuana Party, which wants to legalize pot and end the asinine War on Drugs.

I've been honored to watch transhumanism grow a lot under my candidacy. My main goal all along has been to tell the world that science and technological innovation is coming far more quickly than ever before, and as a nation, we must answer to it with practical and forward-thinking policies. If we don't, it could lead to increased inequality, a blatantly dystopian future, and a severe planetary environmental crisis.

Take the case of genetic editing. China is leading the charge to create designer babies with the tech—including possibly augmenting intelligence and strength—but Clinton and Trump won't touch the subject, instead focusing on sexual harassment and Emailgate. How will they feel in two decades when a new generation of Chinese babies are genetically smarter or stronger than Americans?

Nowhere is the travesty of American politics more clear than in the 2016 presidential debates. Not one major question on climate change, despite it being a huge worry on most everyone's mind. Also, not one question on artificial intelligence, even though my consulting with the US Navy confirms it's one of the most important national security issues of the 21st Century.

On October 19, along with Gary Johnson, Jill Stein, and Evan McMullin, I participated in an online ISideWith debate, where we all addressed the same questions Trump and Clinton were thrown by Chris Wallace in the third debate in real time. It astounded me that no science and technology questions were addressed. Nothing has or will affect the American people more than science and technology. The global average life expectancy has doubled since the start of the last century, and I think it might double again in the next 25 years—dramatically affecting social security, welfare, and healthcare. The internet gave us instant communication in all the corners of the world with all people—making new voting methods possible. And robots are poised to take all jobs by middle of this century—unemploying everyone (probably even the president).

These are not side issues. These are the most pressing concerns in politics—not whether Trump is misogynistic or Clinton lost emails.

For damn sake America, get it together! Those words are the result of my two years of campaigning: disbelief that sane people put up with this presidential game show bullshit. As I told Anonymous a few weeks ago when I interviewed on their podcast: The entire election shitshow is controlled by corporate people in boardrooms and the uber-wealthy. Everything from your media to your voting machines to the shoes you wear to walk outside to vote is part of their creation. You are being led by leaders you dislike and becoming people you don't want to be. That's what American politics has come to. And we all let it happen.

Outside of crowdfunding my Immortality Bus, I have not taken a penny in donations for my presidential campaign. I've made it this way because you can't have honest elections and big money together. On the top of my list for how to make America truly great, is to totally reform campaign finance laws, so that no candidate has an advantage. The second thing to do is reform media coverage. There must be a way to bring minor candidates into the limelight—and not just to sell commercials for media conglomerates, but because candidates have good and new ideas.

Third—and this is a critical—we must include polling of all candidates. I've only been in one semi-poll, an iQuanti report based on Google Trends. It put me 4th in third party candidates. My campaign has been going on for over two full years, with debates, street protests, major media press interviews, etc. And I've only been in just one poll to base my success (or lack of success) on? No wonder the system doesn't change—no one's heard about me, even though I'm a regular major media journalist and public figure in the science and tech world. The government should get in the polling business to make sure third party candidates get regularly polled, so they don't spend all their time and resources trying to establish name recognition.

Finally, if there was one all-important systematic change I'd make to the election process, I'd implement a ranked voting system. This system would allow you to vote third party, but if the vote ended up being meaningless because it wouldn't affect the electoral outcome, it would then go to the next ranked candidate. Tens of millions of Americans dislike Clinton and Trump, but they feel they must vote for one candidate or the other because otherwise they believe their vote will be wasted. A ranked voting system eliminates that.

The 2016 election is not an anomaly. The hate, vitriol, and nausea many of us feel is real. America is a painfully divided nation, and without wide systematic changes in the election process, nothing will change. That change begins with a vote for parties and candidates outside of the two party monopoly America has become. The change also begins by realizing that America is a greedy blind corporate machine, and that like all corporations, the workers can fight back by striking, by protesting, and by making sure their might is felt.

****

35) Revolutionary Politics are Necessary for Transhumanism to Succeed

Now that my hectic presidential campaign is nearly over, I will be attempting to further integrate the US Transhumanist Party into the futurist community. One way I will do this is by leaving my post as chairman and treasurer of the party, and handing operations over to others in the transhumanist community. But before I do so, I want to explain some of my thoughts and controversial decisions of the past two years as its leading officer.

I formed the Transhumanist Party in October 2014 to be a missing link in the transhumanist social movement—a movement which aims to radically improve human beings with technology and also to wage a war of science against biological death. Up until then, transhumanism had been desperately short on organizations with political emphasis and legal bite. The party, as well as my presidential candidacy, went on to receive much media attention, both nationally and internationally. This helped to grow transhumanism, as did the dozen or so international transhumanist parties that soon formed after the US one.

Despite the overwhelming success and recognition of the Transhumanist Party, over the last 25 months, there has been much contention directed by some in the transhumanist community against the US party and my efforts to promote transhumanism—especially via my presidential candidacy. Some have insisted politics and science shouldn't mix. Others have said I was just out to make a name for myself. Some religious transhumanists accused me of doing the Antichrist's work because I adamantly promoted transhumanism with strong secular undertones.

The culmination of this opposition to my work resulted in a community-wide petition in 2015 to disavow my presidential candidacy. For weeks, the document was shared and spammed in social media, especially into the dozens of major transhumanist Facebook groups. While the petition was signed by some notable transhumanist elders, the sheer lack of signatures—first the petition authors wanted to get 1000 signatures, then they lowered it to 100 when they realized so few people were signing it—showed that the great majority in the community were not against my campaign.

After the petition's lack of success, many of my critics in the community took aim at the US Transhumanist Party itself, questioning through social media posts and articles the party's legitimacy and its legality—and whether we were a Federal Election Committee (FEC) approved political party. (We aren't.) Generally, this antagonism came from elder and academic futurists, and not the quickly growing millennial base of transhumanists that now make up the greater part of the movement.

Let me start by saying, under my leadership, the Transhumanist Party has not striven much to be a so-called "legal" political party. I did try to register the party at the FEC headquarters in Washington DC, but an FEC director quickly turned me down. She explained it takes lots of formal paperwork, lots of incorporated state parties, lots of declared federal party candidates, and lots of bank accounts with money in them to become considered to be a FEC-approved political entity.

As I was leaving the building, the director handed me a 100-page plus manual on how to become a political party in America and properly pay my party taxes. The dense book contained precise regulation on everything from food expenses to lobbying parameters to employee salaries. I laughed. On average, the Transhumanist Party receives about $150 a month in donations, and no one at the party has ever been paid a salary, including me.

Perhaps in the future, the Transhumanist Party will be more formal and recognized by the FEC, but under my care, the US party was not concerned much about laws, membership, rules, etiquette, or what espresso expenses we incurred at Starbucks. For me, the Transhumanist Party was a political vehicle mostly designed for a singular purpose: to create a social environment that facilitates expediently conquering human death using science and technology. Such a purpose is to aim for a near total revolution in the human experience. Therefore, the Transhumanist Party, by nature, is a revolutionary party. I soon threw the FEC manual in a trash bin.

With this in mind, any calls from critics during my tenure to make the Transhumanist Party a more traditional and legal political entity were currently were not of high importance. The other revolutions that have taken place in history—caused by the likes of Robespierre, Gandhi, Mandela, and George Washington, to name a few—also did not follow many rules or worry much about legality. Their strength was in exactly that they were beyond the law and beyond what society considered politically correct.

However, when considering political parties, let's not confuse legality with legitimacy. The US Transhumanist Party is entirely legitimate, and has been from the day it was founded, which is partly why it's become so popular around the world. Legitimacy comes from supporters and citizens. It comes from their actions and ideas—and sometimes from the buildings they occupy by force, the hacks they make on adversary's computers, and even the smoking barrels of their guns.

True legitimacy does not come from a governmental agency such as the Federal Election Committee, the IRS, or a judge with a rubber stamp. And it certainly doesn't come from that unreliable, troll-haven Wikipedia, where the Transhumanist Party page was deleted, despite hundreds of major media articles featuring the party as notable.

That said, whether the party and my presidential campaign was consulting with the US Navy, speaking at the World Bank, opening the popular Financial Times Camp Alphaville, doing an AMA on Reddit's Futurology, interviewing with Anonymous, or being included as a notable new party by the US Archives, it certainly did join the ranks of entities that influenced and broadened American politics. The proof is in Google Trends and internet rankings, where the Transhumanist Party is constantly searched for and gets thousands of daily views.

Beyond the question of legitimacy, though, is a more important aspect of the current Transhumanist Party—its adamant public stance that activism and civil disobedience is necessary and desirable. When I publicly said—at least a few times—that the party and I wanted to rewrite parts of the US Constitution, I meant it.

After all, we didn't drive our Immortality Bus across America to deliver a *Transhumanist Bill of Rights* to the US Capitol because we agree with America and its policies. We drove that bus and delivered that document precisely because we disagree. And we did this despite our love of the core of America—because, after all, the USA is an amazing nation. It just can be significantly improved—and should be.

The posting and delivery of the *Transhumanist Bill of Rights* was partially an act of civil disobedience, and I endorse such actions so long as America continues to betray its citizens with deathist policies and regulations endorsed by the past 43 religious US presidents. Nearly 250 years after America was founded, it's finally time we get someone in office who makes decisions and passes laws based entirely on reason and the scientific method. It's impossible for a religious president, a religious Supreme Court, and a 100 percent religious US Congress (all who state they publicly believe in afterlives) to care enough about medical, scientific, and technological progress when they all think they're going to be immortal angels in heaven someday.

You may not agree with that fact. You may think the Transhumanist Party and my own presidential campaign are too extreme. But I assure you that losing a friend to cancer, or a child to a car accident, or one's mind to Alzheimer's justifies our steadfast dedication. In the 21st century, with the resources our country has and the know-how of our amazing scientists and technologists, we can in 25 years' time change all this. We can eliminate most suffering, most disease, and even death for everyone—if we simply would just put all our energy into it. That would be the greatest, most positive revolution in the history of America and of the world.

Whatever happens, no one is forcing the critics in the futurist communities to support the Transhumanist Party. People can go off and form their own parties, support their own candidates, and advocate for whatever they want in their own ways. In fact, I think the more science and technology parties we have, the better.

Politics and minor third parties are a great way to push burgeoning movements like transhumanism forward. Unfortunately, along the way, it's impossible to make everyone happy—and critics and naysayers will be ubiquitous. But if the greater good has been served and progress has been made, then we should acknowledge that entities like the Transhumanist Party—revolutionary or not— have played a helping hand in positively moving the world forward.

****

36) Meet the Futurist Political Parties

The day is coming when designer babies are the norm, space travel is available to everyone, and robots have personhood and even pay taxes. It may not be coming soon, but a number of futurist political parties have emerged in the last few years to make sure we're ready when it does.

The fledgling parties have science fictional names like Transhumanist Party, Space Party, Longevity Party, and Futurist Party. That's just in the US. Overseas, there's Spain's Alianza Futurista, Australia's WikiLeaks Party, Russia's Evolution 2045, and several others.

So far, none of these new political parties have elected anyone to office; they exist mostly on the internet, advocating for issues like universal basic income, life extension research funding, totally free education, mandated green-friendly policies, free and open internet as an inalienable right of online citizens, and support for morphological freedom—the right do with your body whatever you want so long as it doesn't hurt someone else.

Collectively they represent a potential shift in the current political landscape, and its sluggish approach to technological change and forward-thinking ideas. Many people, especially young people, feel it's time to upend the status quo.

Myself included. I founded the US Transhumanist Party in 2014, and then ran as its nominated 2016 US Presidential candidate. I also formed the Transhumanist Party Global, along with Amon Twyman, to give an umbrella network and global constitution to the nearly 25 nationalist Transhumanist Parties spread out over five continents.

To talk more about futurist political movements and achieve some synergy, I recently met with Weston T. von Hochmuth—you may know him as redditor Xenophon1. He helped form the Futurist Party last year, and founded Reddit's Futurology subreddit, which at last look had 10+ million subscribers.

"The Futurist Party is a decentralized, non-hierarchical, and open-source political movement," he told me. "It is one among a community of growing international philosophies founded on an emphasis towards addressing the political interaction with technology: Net Neutrality, Space Industry, and Basic Income to hurt or help the institutions and citizens of the US." The party's supporters are a community unified behind a singular idea: progress in education, economics, and exploration. "Futurists in office, at the polls, and as citizens of the United States stand for these three E's as our keys to the better future," he said.

Weston is in his twenties, and he is part of a changing generation—a generation of millions of gamers, glued to their smartphones, wearing virtual reality headsets and exploring new realities—that feels there's room to change, maybe even revolutionize the current binary political system. But that revolution isn't happening overnight—most future-oriented political parties are still in the infancy stage of development. The Futurist Party, for example, has a website, a presence on various social media sites, and over 5,000 subscribers on its subreddit, but it has yet to organize much outside the online community.

The Space Party, which advocates for more government spending and social support of the space industry, and is generating interest on Facebook, but little has been done in the way of any formal events. "We are only an online movement at this time, but there is a lot of interest," Justin Waters, a law school student who runs the US Space Party website, told me. "I often get emails asking what I can do, and how I can help."

Some parties are purely internet phenomena, but that doesn't mean they won't have any power or influence. The web has a way of sparking grassroots revolutions without ever stepping on the grass. There is power in numbers online.

I've seen this with the Longevity Party, which exists mostly on Facebook with some 7,000 members. While not formally a political party with ambitions to gain office, the Longevity Party has organized small street demonstrations in Brussels, Cambridge, and Washington DC. The members, including one of its well known founders, Maria Konovalenko, used the protests to advocate for more funding into life extension research and an end to "deathist" culture.

And some parties, including the Transhumanist Party, do hope to elect representatives to public office. The UK Transhumanist Party is running a candidate, neuroscience expert Alexander Karran, PhD, for the Labour safe seat of Liverpool Walton in the UK General Election. The party is in the process of printing out and distributing 20,000 propaganda leaflets.

Not everyone is happy with the futurist political movement. Some people have suggested that these groups are too influenced by the Silicon Valley bubble—not exactly representative of America as a whole. I've heard complaints that futurist issues and politics can't mix, and that science and technology should remain untouched by political bias and lobbyist money.

An article in Stanford University's nonpartisan political magazine, Stanford Political Journal summed up the argument this way:

It is difficult to predict which emerging technologies will influence our politics, but the political issues that are bound to arrive must be dealt with by political scientists, theorists, humanist scholars, not by life-extensionists, biohackers, technologists, singularitarians, cyronicists, techno-optimists who are beginning to get involved in the political game.

Many people, including me, disagree. Politics has remained in the hands of a two-party system dominated by lobbyists, lawyers, and professional politicians for far too long. And even though no futurist parties have much chance of winning in elections in the next few years, they are raising awareness about issues that will shape society for the future generations.

Renowned political analyst Roland Benedikter said of the US Transhumanist party:

The Transhumanism movement organized itself for the first time as a concrete political force in the autumn of 2014, thereby reaching a new level of public visibility and potential impact, irrespective of the immediate success it can or will have at the ballots.

Benedikter went on:

In the next ten years everyone is gonna be forced to deal with how we deal with artificial intelligence, everyone is gonna be forced to deal with longevity as people live longer, everyone is gonna be forced to deal with some of the bionics, the chip implants and the mind uploading.

But the public is still hesitant to embrace many of the far-out future concepts bandied around in futurist circles. Franz Eiber, speaker and board member of the German Humanist Party told me:

The technical/science fiction issues are not easy to present to many people in Germany, as many people are afraid of their privacy, and therefore are skeptical against too much technology. For example, the idea of mind uploading is difficult for many people to accept.

Mind uploading—the theoretical process of uploading the human mind and consciousness to a computer—is a thorny issue, and presents a wide array of political conundrums. Some experts believe it could be here in as little as 20 years, and if so, what will we call a person living in a machine? A human being? Or something else? And what country does he, or she, or it belong to? Can it procreate and multiply itself thousands of times? And then, can it also vote? Futurist parties want address these questions and create policies to prepare for them.

"We collectively support mind uploading as possibly the ultimate form of long-term survival," Sergio Tarrero, president of the small Alianza Futurista transhumanist political party in Spain, told me. "And, of course, that consciousness should have full voting rights."

Optimism aside, the real question remains: What can a bunch of minor third parties hope to accomplish on their own? History has been filled with third parties going nowhere. A cursory search of past and current political parties in the United States reveals dozens that no one has ever heard of, and of course that list doesn't include the potentially hundreds of fringe parties not listed in Wikipedia.

But futurist parties might have a distinct advantage in the next few decades that help them rise to prominence. This advantage is emerging technology itself, which could potentially change the political landscape even before small futurist parties making their way through the traditional system.

One idea being floated around by futurists is "real-time democracy" (also called Direct Digital Democracy), where citizens can vote on legislative bills and agendas online, or even right from their smartphones. If this type of technology appeals to the younger generation, it could give futurist parties an advantage in the polls, or encourage more young people to vote.

Other more radical technologies on the horizon may also prove useful for futurist parties. Futurists, including myself, have asked if perhaps selfless artificial intelligences in robot bodies would be better suited for running the government. Yet others hope to see virtual nations like Bitnation or Zero State, which supports a boundaryless community that could operate entirely like its own country, using emerging tech like cryptocurrency, virtual reality, solar power, and Blockchain technology, which some claim could revolutionize voting.

Over the last six months, I've corresponded with various leaders of futurist political parties in an attempt to consolidate a political platform that we all share. One thing I discovered is that while we are small now as a political community, the possibility of becoming much larger is very real. With a united front, we might be able to push ourselves to a type of prominence enjoyed by other large third political parties, like the Libertarian Party or the Green Party. The future isn't relegated to just one side of the aisle.

****

37) Why I'm Running for California Governor as a Libertarian

My thirties started off in countries ravaged by environmental destruction and dictatorships. Back then, I was a journalist for National Geographic, spending most of my time abroad, even though I still called Los Angeles—my birth city—home. In the 100+ countries I visited, I reported on some harrowing stories: the Killing Fields in Cambodia, the near total deforestation of Paraguay, and the tense nuclear stand-off between India and Pakistan. I always hoped my words and on-camera television commentary brought some sanity and peace to the chaos.

While on assignment in Vietnam near the demilitarized zone, a near-miss with a landmine that could have been catastrophic sent me back home to the safety of the United States. Desiring stability, I started a real-estate development business with capital saved from my journalism. America was booming and my business thrived. I soon sold most of my real-estate portfolio, allowing me to live off my long-term investments.

I was lucky, for sure. Only a year later, I watched America, its banking system, and its real-estate market collapse. I watched friends lose everything, and my government try to fix something it had partially caused. The lessons—the distrust of big government, crony capitalism and unmanageable debt—seared themselves into my value system.

Like many entrepreneurs, I became a libertarian because of one simple concept: reason. It just made sense to embrace a philosophy that promotes maximum freedom and personal accountability. "Hands off" was my motto—and in business, if you wanted to succeed, those words are sacred. But "hands off" applies to more than just good entrepreneurial economics. It applies to social life, politics, culture, religion, and especially how innovation occurs.

I've been a passionate science and technology guy—an advocate of radical innovation—ever since I can remember. In college, I focused on the ethics and challenges of science for my Philosophy degree. But my stories for National Geographic and my witnessing of the Great Recession viscerally reminded me that government and the growing fundamentalism in Congress was desperately trying to control innovation and progress—even at the expense of people's health, safety, and prosperity. With plenty of free time after the sale of my business to mount a challenge, I decided to use my writing skills to fight this backward thinking.

I began penning *The Transhumanist Wager*, a philosophical novel published in 2013 that blasts Luddism. The controversial libertarian-minded manifesto has now been compared to Ayn Rand's work hundreds of times in reviews—though I often point out my book is quite different to *Atlas Shrugged*. Nonetheless, the popularity of my novel thrust me into the radical science and tech movement as a public figure, whose main hub was right where I live in the San Francisco Bay area.

Looking for a way to take science and technology into the political realm, I decided to make a run for the U.S. presidency in 2016 as the self-described "science candidate." I knew I couldn't win the election, but it was a great way to awaken many Americans to the desperate plight of our country's increasingly stifled science and innovation sector. My experience in media has helped propel my candidacy. I spoke at the World Bank, appeared on The Joe Rogan Experience podcast, was interviewed by the hacker collective Anonymous, and consulted for the U.S. Navy about technology, among other things. Even 2016 Libertarian nominee Gary Johnson invited me to interview as his possible vice president. Alone in his New Mexico house, we talked shop for 24 hours solid. He chose Governor Bill Weld as his VP, but I left Johnson knowing I would soon be making a stand for the Libertarian Party.

Due to the fact I was arguably the first visible science presidential candidate in American history, I ran a very centric, science and tech-oriented platform, one that was designed to be as inclusive of as many political lines as possible. With leadership comes some compromise, and I veered both right and left to try to satisfy as many people as I could, even when it meant going against some of my own personal opinions. I believe a politician represents the people, and he or she must never forget that—or forget the honor that such a task carries.

One thing I didn't stray from was my belief that everything could be solved best by the 'scientific method'—the bastion of reason that says a thing or idea works only if you can prove it again and again via objective, independent evaluation. I'll always be a pragmatic rationalist, and reason to me is the primary motivator when considering how to tackle problems, social or otherwise. I continue to passionately believe in the promise of using reason, science and technology to better California and the world. After all, the standard of living has been going up around the globe because of a singular factor: more people have access to new science and technology than ever before. Nothing moves the world forward like innovation does.

Yet, in the political climate of 2017, few things seem more at risk as innovation. A conservative, religious government stands to overwhelm California with worries about radical tech and science, such as implementing Federal regulation that stifles artificial intelligence, driverless cars, stem cells, drones, and genetic editing.

Sadly, the same could be said of immigration, women's rights, and environmental issues. Then there's America's move towards expanding its already overly expensive military, which you and I pay for out of our pockets so that generals can fight far-off wars. America can do better than this. California can do better than this.

And we must. After all, the world is changing—and changing quite dramatically. Even libertarians like me face the real possibility that capitalism and job competition—which we always advocated for—won't survive into the next few decades because of widespread automation and the proliferation of robot workers. Then there's the burgeoning dilemma of cyber security and unwanted tracking of the technology that citizens use. And what of augmenting intelligence via genetic editing—something the Chinese are leading the charge on, but most Americans seem too afraid to try? In short, what can be done to ensure the best future?

Much can be done. And I believe it can all be done best via a libertarian framework, which is precisely why I am declaring my run for 2018 California governor. We need leadership that is willing to use radical science, technology, and innovation—what California is famous for—to benefit us all. We need someone with the nerve to risk the tremendous possibilities to save the environment through bioengineering, to end cancer by seeking a vaccine or a gene-editing solution for it, to embrace startups that will take California from the world's 7th largest economy to maybe even the largest economy—bigger than the rest of America altogether. And believe me when I say this is possible: artificial intelligence and genetic editing will become some of the first multi-trillion dollar businesses in the near future.

We can do this, California, and it doesn't have to be through blue or red political parties, which have left many of us aghast at the current world. It can be done through the libertarian philosophy of embracing all that is the most inventive and unbridled in us—and letting that pave the way forward. A challenging future awaits us, but we can meet it head on and lead the way not just for California and America, but for all of humanity.

****

38) The Future of Libertarianism Could be Radically Different

Many societies and social movements operate under a foundational philosophy that often can be summed up in a few words. Most famously, in much of the Western world, is the Golden Rule: Do onto others as you want them to do to you. In libertarianism, the backbone of the political philosophy is the non-aggression principle (NAP). It argues it's immoral for anyone to use force against another person or their property except in cases of self-defense.

A challenge has recently been posed to the non-aggression principle. The thorny question libertarian transhumanists are increasingly asking in the 21st century is: Are so-called natural acts or occurrences immoral if they cause people to suffer? After all, taken to a logical philosophical extreme, cancer, aging, and giant asteroids arbitrarily crashing into the planet are all aggressive, forceful acts that harm the lives of humans.

Traditional libertarians throw these issues aside, citing natural phenomena as unable to be morally forceful. This thinking is supported by most people in Western culture, many of whom are religious and fundamentally believe only God is aware and in total control of the universe. However, transhumanists—many who are secular like myself—don't care about religious metaphysics and whether the universe is moral. (It might be, with or without an almighty God.) What transhumanists really care about are ways for our parents to age less, to make sure our kids don't die from leukemia, and to save the thousands of species that vanish from Earth every year due to rising temperatures and the human-induced forces.

An impasse has developed among philosophers, and questions once thought absurd, now bear the cold bearing of reality. For example, automation, robots, and software may challenge if not obliterate capitalism as we know it before the 21st century is out. Should libertarians stand against it and develop tenets and safeguards to protect their livelihoods? I have argued, yes, a universal basic income of some sort to guarantee a suitable livelihood is in philosophical line with the non-aggression principle.

However, it's more of a stretch to talk about the NAP in terms of healthcare. Nonetheless, the same new rules could apply. Libertarian transhumanists believe aging is a negative force—something that we did not invite into our lives. Given that lifespans already doubled in the 20th century due to medicine and technology, and may double again for the same reasons in the 21st century, do we begin to see aging—and even dying—as an unwanted and so-called immoral force against our very lives?

I believe we do. In fact, in my run for the governor of California as a libertarian, a main policy of mine is to label aging as a disease. The classification takes this universal phenomenon and reduces it to exactly what it is: an aggressive force that I do want in my life.

Knowing my arguments, my libertarian friends have asked if I would use government resources to help fight against aging. As a libertarian, I would prefer the private industry to tackle this problem. However, as an aspiring politician in the real world, I understand that when our government and National Institute of Health (NIH) classifies something as a disease, the entire world notices, and often billions of dollars flows into the research to tackle it. I'm not sure about billions of tax dollars being appropriate, but I'm sure I'd want the government stamp of approval—as the people's stamp of approval—on it, making clear that it's an important issue.

I think support for some government help with the fighting of diseases is warranted, if only to be symbolic in support. In my opinion, and to most transhumanist libertarians, death and aging are enemies of the people and of liberty (perhaps the greatest ones), similar to foreign invaders running up our shores. Therefore, I think government and libertarians have some interest in stepping in to protect life and liberties in this case, as they would against foreign aggression.

I'd also argue some government help for the space industry is also warranted. After all, not being able to get humans off this planet easily poses a major existential risk in the event of a global plague, major asteroid hit, or some other catastrophic event. In this case again, a coordinated minarchist state effort against a foreign enemy threatening life, liberty, and country could be acceptable—and not too far of a stretch for some libertarians.

In the end, I'm glad I'm running for governor in California, as I suspect the majority of libertarians will be hesitant at looking at the non-aggression principle in this way. And California has a way of allowing these strange ideas to get the green light and grow. And why shouldn't it? Anything that harms the human being and its ability to thrive is an affront our very lives and values. In the 21st century, we should rise up and use everything within our means to increase the success of our very lives.

****

39) The Problem with the Libertarian Party

As someone guided by the ways of science—my holy grail is the Scientific Method—I try to stay focused on realistic probabilities of what's achievable. This carries over into my libertarian candidacy for California Governor, and while I'd like to win in 2018, I know it's all but impossible.

Some libertarians are angry that I publicly admit I won't win. But this is the quintessential problem with the Libertarian Party—many members I've met are unrealistic. After a year of attending conferences, executive committee meetings, and party functions, I've come to realize a significant number of libertarians seem downright delusional when it comes to politics.

It's really not surprising libertarians almost never do well in elections. Most libertarian candidates have little public standing, resources, or professional acumen. What pains me is despite this, many in the Libertarian Party will incessantly and often belligerently shout from the rooftops how we are going to win our political races—and how current government and its institutions are appalling and blatantly abusive. They insist that "taxation is theft," or forcing people to get drivers licenses is oppressive, or not being allowed to have an armed tank parked in one's front yard is proof Americans live under a tyrannical government.

I notice many libertarians—especially the loudest ones—don't have much education, managerial experience, or money. I suspect they don't realize what it's like to own a half-million dollar home with a mortgage, and then have one's neighbor park an armed tank on the front lot, reducing the neighborhood's entire value. I'm not against people owning tanks, but America did not become the wealthiest, most powerful nation in the world through such antics. Freedom is one thing—disregard for basic neighborly cooperation and social precedent is another. This is a major problem with libertarians. They are often so fringe, they hardly know how to get along with each other, let alone the general public. Ironically, it's very rare to meet a libertarian who actually thinks another libertarian is "libertarian" enough.

Beyond many libertarians' obsessiveness on all matters of freedom lies a far more ineffective way of being. The Libertarian Party prides itself on being the "The Party of Principle"—and its members act so much upon that idea that while their biggest aim is freedom, they have unwittingly become a highly closed-minded political group. Many libertarians actually believe their ideas are perfect—and their policies cannot be compromised or altered. As a result, there is little change possible in their platforms. Those platforms have, after almost 50 years of being a political party, done almost nothing for them in terms of the one thing that matters: winning elections to cause change in their worlds. Libertarians hold no governorships or seats in the US Congress, despite being the 3rd largest party in America.

Politics is a contact sport that is always changing. To win, you need to evolve, adapt, and sometimes set out anew. The libertarians seem to want nothing of this. Despite growing inequality, increased dependence on the government, and jobs being threatened by technology, they insist nothing should be done that adjusts the libertarian philosophical status quo. They insist they already have all the answers. And for some, those answers are a complete reset of the government, or even disbanding Federal institutions entirely— despite the practical impossibility of such things because of the structure of Congress and the other branches of US government.

It's for this reason, that big ticket donors or major media pays little or no attention to libertarians. As a former National Geographic journalist and correspondent for *The New York Times*, it's easy to see why libertarians are rarely covered. This point was made abundantly clear to me when Larry Sharpe, a well-liked figure in the Libertarian Party, all but endorsed another libertarian candidate for governor in California, Nickolas Wildstar. Multiple candidates running for the same office within the same party are a fact of life, but when Sharpe jubilantly pointed to Wildstar at a recent public event and said: "There is a future for California that is not the same old thing…it's this man right here…Wildstar is the right answer for the future of this state," I had to do a double take and roll my eyes.

California is the world's 6th largest economy with nearly 40 million residents. More billionaires live here than any other territory in the world. Its universities boast one of the highest amount of Nobel prize winners anywhere. According to Wildstar's campaign biography, he hasn't even been to college. He also doesn't list any notable business experience, executive leadership history, or credible political qualifications. Apparently, Mr. Wildstar, an unknown rapper with a tiny social media presence, simply woke up one day and wanted to become governor of America's most populated state. It's simply unimaginable that libertarians could expect to be taken realistically by the public when they support candidates who aren't qualified to run for minor office, let alone the most important and powerful job in California.

It's this kind of unreasonableness, being spread from the top of the Libertarian Party all the way down to an army of anarchist trolls on Facebook, that has made it the laughing stock of politics. In order for libertarians to be taken seriously, and possibly win some elections someday, they must ban together and get a hold on reality. They must not accept just any candidate reciting the party line who decides one day they want to lead multi-trillion dollar economies and tens of millions of citizens.

Nickolas Sarawak, Chairman of the Libertarian Party, has the well-wishing goal of running 2000 libertarian candidates in the upcoming 2018 elections. But I fear this strategy will only highlight one thing if the candidates are not qualified or reputable: that the Libertarian Party has no interest in ever challenging the Democrat and GOP duopoly in a meaningful way. I would much rather see the Libertarian Party focus on 100 good candidates across the nation that are important enough to make the news regularly and could possibly impact their respective races.

The Libertarian Party seems to think it matters that there is a libertarian candidate to check-off on in every election. They believe it's good name recognition to be on every ballot—even the smallest political race across the country. Obviously, that's correct to a degree, but far more important is to get a few dozen good candidates across the nation whose public personas stretch far outside the libertarian base, so as to actually help enlarge the party and is goals. For this, those candidates must be reputable public figures with standout resumes, able to actually be seen by the public and media as possible and capable high office holders.

In its quest to protect the freedom of Americans and reduce the size of the government, libertarians have forgotten a core part about politics: being liked. I sometimes call up libertarians on the phone, and when they don't recognize my number, they often answer hostilely: "Who is this? How did you get my damn number?"

This is not the way libertarians are going to win elections, by being socially inept or cantankerous—or by being dreamers. Libertarians will win by pushing forth ideas of limited government and personal freedom with behavior that's more professional and likeable then the Democrats and the Republicans. Libertarians should take a hard look at how diplomacy works, and why the art of friendliness and compromise is often the best platform for building new relationships and winning elections. Libertarians should also come down to Earth with their expectations—and focus on what they can actually accomplish in politics. Otherwise, the Libertarian Party will soon turn 50, and another tiring half century will follow of indefinite losses and ridicule.

****

CHAPTER V: THE PROVOCATUER

40) The Privacy Enigma: Liberty Might be Better Served by Doing Away with Privacy

The constant onslaught of new technology is making our lives more public and trackable than ever, which understandably scares a lot of people. Part of the dilemma is how we interpret the right to privacy using centuries-old ideals handed down to us by our forbearers. I think the 21st century idea of privacy—like so many other taken-for-granted concepts—may need a revamp.

When James Madison wrote the Fourth Amendment—which helped legally establish US privacy ideals and protection from unreasonable search and seizure—he surely wasn't imagining Elon Musk's neural lace, artificial intelligence, the internet, or virtual reality. Madison wanted to make sure government couldn't antagonize its citizens and overstep its governmental authority, as monarchies and the Church had done for centuries in Europe.

For many decades, the Fourth Amendment has mostly done its job. But privacy concerns in the 21st century go way beyond search and seizure issues: Giant private companies like Google, Apple, and Facebook are changing our sense of privacy in ways the government never could. And many of us have plans to continue to use more new tech; one day, many of us will use neural prosthetics and brain implants. These brain-to-machine interfaces will likely eventually lead to the hive mind, where everyone can know each other's precise whereabouts and thoughts at all times, because we will all be connected to each other through the cloud. Privacy, broadly thought of as essential to a democratic society, might disappear.

"While privacy has long been considered a fundamental right, it has never been an inherent right," Jeremy Rifkin, an American economic and social theorist, wrote in *The Zero Marginal Cost Society*. "Indeed, for all of human history, until the modern era, life was lived more or less publicly, as befits most species on Earth."

The question of whether privacy needs to change is really a question of functionality. Is privacy actually useful for individuals or for society? Does having privacy make humanity better off? Does privacy raise the standard of living for the average person?

In some ways, these questions are futile. Technological innovation is already calling the shots, and considering the sheer amount of new tech being bought and used, most people seem content with the more public, transparent world it's ushering in. Hundreds of millions of people willingly use devices and tech that can monitor them, including personal home assistants, credit cards, smartphones, and even pacemakers (in Ohio, a suspect's own pacemaker data will be used in the trial against him.) Additionally, cameras in cities are ubiquitous; tens of thousands of fixed cameras are recording every second of the day, making a walk outside one's own home a trackable affair. Even my new car knows where I'm at and calls me on the car intercom if it feels it's been hit or something suspicious is happening.

Because of all this, in the not so distant future—perhaps as little as 15 years—I imagine a society where everybody can see generally where anyone else is at any moment. Many companies already have some of this ability through the tech we own, but it's not in the public's hands yet to control.

For many, this constant state of being monitored is concerning. But consider that much of our technology can also look right back into the government's world with our own spying devices and software. It turns out Big Brother isn't so big if you're able to track his every move.

The key with such a reality is to make sure government is engulfed by ubiquitous transparency too. Why shouldn't our government officials be required to be totally visible to us all, since they've chosen public careers? Why shouldn't we always know what a police officer is saying or doing, or be able to see not only when our elected Senator meets with lobbyists, but what they say to them?

For better or worse, we can already see the beginnings of an era of in which nothing is private: WikiLeaks has its own transparency problems and has a scattershot record of releasing documents that appear to be politically motivated, but nonetheless has exposed countless political emails, military wires, and intel documents that otherwise would have remained private or classified forever. There is an ongoing battle about whether police body camera footage should be public record. Politicians and police are being videotaped by civilians with cell phones, drones, and planes.

But it's not just government that's a worry. It's also important that people can track companies, like Google, Apple, and Facebook that create much of the software that tracks individuals and the public. This is easier said than done, but a vibrant start-up culture and open-source technology is the antidote. There will always be people and hackers that insist on tracking the trackers, and they will also lead the entrepreneurial crusade to keep big business in check with new ways of monitoring their behavior. There are people hacking and cracking big tech's products to see what their capabilities are and to uncover surreptitious surveillance and security vulnerabilities. This spirit must extend to monitoring all of big tech's activities. Massive openness must become a two-way street.

And I'm hopeful it will, if disappearing privacy trends continue their trajectory, and if technology continues to connect us omnipresently (remember the hive mind?). We will eventually come to a moment in which all communications and movements are public by default.

In such a world, everyone will be forced to be more honest, especially Washington. No more backdoor special interest groups feeding money to our lawmakers for favors. And there would be fewer incidents like Governor Chris Christie believing he can shut down public beaches and then use them himself without anyone finding out. The recent viral photo—taken by a plane overhead—of him bathing on a beach he personally closed is a strong example of why a non-private society has merit.

If no one can hide, then no one can do anything wrong without someone else knowing. That may allow a better, more efficient society with more liberties than the protection privacy accomplishes.

This type of future, whether through cameras, cell phone tracking, drones, implants, and a myriad of other tech could literally shape up America, quickly stopping much crime. Prisons would eventually likely mostly empty, and dangerous neighborhoods would clean up—instead of putting people in jail, we can track them with drones until their sentence is up. Our internet of things devices will call the cops when domestic violence disputes arrive (it was widely reported—but not confirmed—that a smarthome device called the police when a man was allegedly brandishing a gun and beating his girlfriend. Such cases will eventually become commonplace.)

A society lacking privacy would have plenty of liberty-creating phenomena too, likely ushering in an era similar to the 60s where experimental drugs, sex, and artistic creation thrived. Openness, like the vast internet itself, is a facilitator of freedom and personal liberties. A less private society means a more liberal one where unorthodox individuals and visionaries—all who can no longer be pushed behind closed doors—will be accepted for who or what they are.

Like the Heisenberg principle, observation, changes reality. So does a lack of walls between you and others. A radical future like this would bring an era of freedom and responsibility back to humanity and the individual. We are approaching an era where the benefits of a society that is far more open and less private will lead to a safer, diverse, more empathetic world. We should be cautious, but not afraid.

****

41) A Post-Earther Perspective: Environmentalists are Wrong, Nature isn't Sacred

On a warming planet bearing scars of significant environmental destruction, you'd think one of the 21st Century's most notable emerging social groups—transhumanists—would be concerned. Many are not. Transhumanists first and foremost want to live indefinitely, and they are outraged at the fact their bodies age and are destined to die. They blame their biological nature, and dream of a day when DNA is replaced with silicon and data.

Their enmity of biology goes further than just their bodies. They see Mother Earth as a hostile space where every living creature—be it a tree, insect, mammal, or virus—is out for itself. Everything is part of the food chain, and subject to natural law: consumption by violent murder in the preponderance of cases. Life is vicious. It makes me think of pet dogs and cats, and how it's reported they sometimes start eating their owner after they've died.

Many transhumanists want to change all this. They want to rid their worlds of biology. They favor concrete, steel, and code. Where once biological evolution was necessary to create primates and then modern humans, conscious and directed evolution has replaced it. Planet Earth doesn't need iniquitous natural selection. It needs premeditated moral algorithms conceived by logic that do the most good for the largest number of people. This is something that an AI will probably be better at than humans in less than two decade's time.

Ironically, fighting the makings of utopia is a coup a half century in the making. Starting with the good-intentioned people at Greenpeace in the 1970s but overtaken recently with enviro-socialists who often seem to want to control every aspect of our lives, environmentalism has taken over political and philosophical discourse and direction at the most powerful levels of society. Green believers want to make you think humans are destroying our only home, Planet Earth—and that this terrible action of ours is the most important issue of our time. They have sounded a call to "save the earth" by trying to stomp out capitalism and dramatically downsizing our carbon footprint.

The most important issue of our time is actually the evolution of technology, and environmentalists are mistaken in thinking the Earth is our only or permanent home. Before the century is out, our home for much intelligent life will likely be the microprocessor. We will merge with machines and explore both the virtual and physical universe as sentient robots. That's the obvious destiny of our species and the coming AI age, popularized by past and present thinkers like Stephen Hawking, Ray Kurzweil, and Homo Deus author Yuval Noah Harari. Hundred million dollar companies in California led by billionaires like Elon Musk are already working on technology to directly to connect our brains in real time to the internet. We may soon not need the planet at all, just servers and a power source like solar or fusion.

Even if we somehow don't merge with machines (because scared governments outlaw it, for example), we will still use the microprocessor and its data crunching capabilities to change our genetic make-up so dramatically, that it could not be called: natural. We will enter the Star Wars age where we literally change our DNA and biological appearance to become alien and creature-like—to fit whatever environment we need to fit. If this sounds crazy, just consider the Chinese geneticist who last year changed a girl's genes in utero, creating the first alleged designer baby.

Whatever we become—as a former journalist for the National Geographic Channel who has passionately covered many environmental stories—I want to first make it clear what I think humans are doing to the Earth. I do believe we are destroying the environment. I do think we are overpopulated in many cities. I also believe there is high likelihood humans are helping to cause climate change. And while I do think we should not needlessly destroy the planet (especially wildlife) or live in man-made polluted wastelands, the last thing we need to do is put the brakes on consumption, procreation, and progress.

What we're doing to the planet is not as important as what we are achieving as a species in the nearing of transition to the transhumanist age. We will save and improve far more lives in the future via bioengineering, geoengineering, and coming technology than damaged ecosystems across the planet will harm. Salvation is in science and progress, not sustainability or preserving the Earth. To argue or do otherwise is to be sadistic and act immorally against humanity's well-being.

Besides, the envisioned transhumanist future is not just a place where humans can live without the constant threats and hostility of a biological world, it's an age where sentient beings can finally overcome pain and misery. Beyond shedding our terminal flesh and living indefinitely, a secondary goal of the transhuman movement is to overcome all or the majority of suffering—both for ourselves and other nonhuman animals. This is why some believe transhumanism—even if it's made up of post-earthers—is the most humanitarian movement out there.

The tools transhumanists use—science, technology, and reason—to accomplish its watershed aims rely on thriving economies, free markets, and innovation. These mostly come from competitive countries trying to become powerful and make money—a lot of it. Increased economic output is nearly always responsible for raising the standard of living, something that has been going up a lot in the last 50 years for just about every nation on Earth. But that could change quickly as governments increasingly enforce strict pro-environmental regulation which slows down industry and commerce. When you force companies to operate inefficiently for lofty ideals, it hurts their bottom lines, and that in turn hurts workers and everyday people. It's a well-known fact that when economies slow down, people increasingly lose property, turn to violence, and put having families on hold.

But the media usually doesn't paint environmental policy this way. In fact, the media is responsible for a lot of the misinformation propping up the environmental movement, which is often at odds with transhumanism. A typical news headline reads: *Billionaires and Politicians Trying to Protect the Planet.* I have to chuckle. Billionaires and politicians usually have power-hungry ambitions. In general, they don't want people to have access to their wealth, power, or pristine environments—because they want it for themselves. That's why they want walls, borders, ownership, and control of it all. How many people without the resources to even afford housing, healthcare, and food will ever take a vacation to protected land, even if the land is public like a national park. How many hundreds of millions of people in inner cities ever go visit "nature"? They don't.

Modern environmentalism is a fabricated deceit of and for the rich and powerful. It's especially prominent in liberal places like New York City and my home town San Francisco. Sadly, environmentalism is often just a terrible tool to wield power over those of lesser means. The amount of minorities that visit US national parks—only 22 percent—compared to whites is totally out of whack.

Despite the imperfections of capitalism, I continue to support it because it remains the best hope for the poor to improve their standard of life—because at least the individually poor can work hard, be smart, and eventually become rich themselves. This rags to riches phenomenon is not something that can happen in socialist or communist environments, where nearly everyone loses (except the corrupt)—and those losses often lead to starvation and eventual civil war.

Enviro-socialists and their green new deals are some of the worst examples of those trying to bring change about to society. These people produce very little—rarely enough to improve society in any meaningful way—and they promise a pristine planet oblivious to the fact the great majority of people will be harmed, not helped, by such economy-killing policies.

However, there is an alternative to this ugly duopoly system we exist in for the masses. Let's harness the capitalists and use our nation's natural resources to end poverty, spread equality, and get humans to the transhuman age where science will make us all healthier and stronger. America has approximately 150 trillion dollars of uninhabited Federal Land not including national parks that we could divide up among its citizens—that's a half million dollars in net worth of resources to every American—all 325 million of them. As a nation, let's sell this federal land or preferably lease it to the capitalists and corporations who can pay us something in return—a permanent universal basic income, for example. Some call this a Federal Land Dividend. Leased properly, our Federal Land could provide over $1500 a month to every US citizen, giving a household of four $75,000 a year indefinitely.

Naysayers will say the capitalists will forever destroy the land and resources. But over a quarter century, this is unlikely, since all the new capital and innovation from divesting the land will push us far more quickly in the nanotechnology era—an age where we can recreate environments as we please, including those that are destroyed. If you think making plastic with oil is nifty, just wait till we create whole mature forests and jungles in a week's time with coming genetic editing techniques. Also, we'll be able to regrow any animal or plant—including extinct ones—in mass in a laboratory, something that is already on the verge of happening.

But why create the same nature that is so quintessentially cruel, especially as we become transhumans, with perfectly functioning ageless bionic organs and implants in our brains connecting us to the cloud. Let's us create new environments that fit our modern needs. These will be virtual, synthetic, and machines worlds. These new worlds will be far more moral and humanitarian than that of nature. They will be like our homes, cars, and apartments, where everything in it is inanimate or no longer living, and that's why we find sanctuary and comfort in it. If you doubt this, spend a night in the jungle or forest without any comforts or amenities, and see if you survive.

I don't believe in evil, per se, but if there was such a thing, it would be nature—a monster of arbitrary living entities consuming and devouring each other simply to survive. No omnipotent person would ever have the hate in them to create a system where everything wants and needs to sting, eat, and outdo everything else just to live. And yet, that's essentially what the environment is to all living entities. Environmentalists want you to believe nature is sacred and a perfect balance of living things thriving off one another. Nonsense—it's a world war of all life fighting agony and loss—of fight or flight, of death today or death tomorrow for you and your offspring.

It's time to use science and technology to create something better than an environment of biological nature. This begins with admitting the green do-gooder environmentalists are philosophically wrong— and the coming transhumanist age will usher in a world with far less suffering, death, and destruction, even if we have to harm the planet to first get there. Humans must cast off nature, and then they will finally be free of its ubiquitous hostility, misery, and fatalism. Let's rise above the cultural push of environmentalism, because it's antithetical to our future.

****

42) Will Licensing Parents Save Children's Lives & Improve Society?

A few years ago, I was at a doctor party, the kind where tired residents drop by in their scrubs, everyone drinks red wine, and discussion centers around medical industry gripes. I wandered over to a group of obstetricians and listened in. One tall blonde woman said something that caught my attention: with 10,000 kids dying everyday around the world from starvation, you'd think we'd put birth control in the water.

The philosophical conundrum of controlling human procreation rests mostly on whether all human beings are actually responsible enough to be good parents and can provide properly for their offspring. Clearly, untold numbers of children -- for example, those millions that are slaves in the illegal human trafficking industry -- are born to unfit parents.

In an attempt to solve this problem and give hundreds of millions of future kids a better life, I cautiously endorse the idea of licensing parents, a process that would be little different than getting a driver's license. Parents who pass a series of basic tests qualify and get the green light to get pregnant and raise children. Those applicants who are deemed unworthy -- perhaps because they are homeless, or have hard drug problems, or are violent criminals, or have no resources to raise a child properly and keep it from going hungry -- would not be allowed until they could demonstrate they were suitable parents.

Transhumanist Hank Pellissier, founder of the Brighter Brains Institute, also supports the idea, insisting on humanitarian grounds that it would bring a measured sense of responsibility to raising kids. In an essay, he notes professor and bioethics pioneer Joseph Fletcher saying that "many births are accidental". Accidentally getting pregnant often leaves women unable to pursue their careers and lives as they might've hoped for and wanted.

Naturally, some environmentalists, such as American educator Paul L Ehrlich, author of landmark book *The Population Bomb*, also advocate for government intervention to control human population, which would be one sure way to help the planet's fragile and depleted ecosystems.

One of the most comprehensive works about the idea of restricting breeding is Peg Tittle's book *Should Parents be Licensed? Debating the Issues*. It's a balanced collection of essays by experts with various views on the subject.

There's no question that some of the ideas of licensing parents make sense. After all, we don't allow people to drive cars on crack cocaine. Why would we allow them to procreate if they want while on it? The goal with licensing parents is not so much to restrict freedoms, but to guarantee the maximum resources to those children that exist and will exist in the future.

Of course, the problem is always in the details. How could society monitor such a licensing process? Would governments force abortion upon mothers if they were found to be pregnant without permission? These things seem unimaginable in most societies around the world. Besides, who wants the government handling human breeding when it can't do basic things like balance its own budgets and stay out of wars? Perhaps a nonprofit entity like the World Health Organization might be able to step in and offer more confidence. I also like the ideas of local communities stepping in to facilitate this idea amongst themselves.

The sad fact is that many children born into poverty end up costing taxpayers billions. Despite all this money spent, a high percentage of those same kids will end up on the streets, in gangs, or in prison after they become adults. With that mind, just as legalization of abortion has helped drive down crime rates, licensing parents would likely have the same effect.

The approximate 10,000 starving child deaths a day that that the aforementioned doctor cited come from various reports and studies, all of which point to the fact that well over 50 million kids have died due to hunger and malnutrition in the last 30 years. That's a lot of kids.

What's more, 15 percent of kids in the US -- the supposed wealthiest country in the world -- suffer from hunger. A large portion of them are born to families that don't have the resources to properly raise a child. After all, if you can't feed a child, you probably shouldn't have one. Licensing would've restricted many of those births until the parents were more able to deal with the challenges of procreation, which is undoubtedly the most intense and serious long term responsibility most human beings will face in their lives.

As a liberty-loving person, I have always eschewed giving up any freedoms. However, in some cases, the statistics are so overwhelming, that at the very least, given the coming era of indefinite lifespans and transhumanist technology, we must remain open-minded to consider how best to move the species forward to produce the happiest and healthiest children for the planet.

Anything less will leave us with millions more preventable deaths and incalculable suffering of innocent kids.

****

43) When Does Hindering Life Extension Science Become a Crime?

Every human being has both a minimum and a maximum amount of life hours left to live. If you add together the possible maximum life hours of every living person on the planet, you arrive at a special number: the optimum amount of time for our species to evolve, find happiness, and become the most that it can be. Many reasonable people feel we should attempt to achieve this maximum number of life hours for humankind. After all, very few people actually wish to prematurely die or wish for their fellow humans' premature deaths.

In a free and functioning democratic society, it's the duty of our leaders and government to implement laws and social strategies to maximize these life hours that we want to safeguard. Regardless of ideological, political, religious, or cultural beliefs, we expect our leaders and government to protect our lives and ensure the maximum length of our lifespans. Any other behavior cuts short the time human beings have left to live. Anything else becomes a crime of prematurely ending human lives. Anything else fits the common legal term we have for that type of reprehensible behavior: criminal manslaughter.

In 2001, former President George W. Bush restricted federal funding for stem cell research, one of the most promising fields of medicine in the 21st Century. Stem cells can be used to help fight disease and, therefore, can lengthen lives. Bush restricted the funding because his conservative religious beliefs—some stem cells came from aborted fetuses—conflicted with his fiduciary duty of helping millions of ailing, disease-stricken human beings. Much medical research in the United States relies heavily on government funding and the legal right to do the research. Ultimately, when a disapproving President limits public resources for a specific field of science, the research in that field slows down dramatically—even if that research would obviously lengthen and improve the lives of millions.

It's not just politicians that are prematurely ending our lives with what can be called "pro-death" policies and ideologies. In 2009, on a trip to Africa, Pope Benedict XVI told journalists that the epidemic of AIDS would be worsened by encouraging people to use condoms. More than 25 million people have died from AIDS since the first cases began being reported in the news in the early 1980s. In numerous studies, condoms have been shown to help stop the spread of HIV, the virus that causes AIDS. This makes condoms one of the simplest and most affordable life extension tools on the planet. Unfathomably, the billion-person strong Catholic Church actively supports the idea that condom usage is sinful, despite the fact that such a malicious policy has helped sicken and kill a staggering amount of innocent people.

Hank Pellissier, a futurist and organizer of the conference Transhuman Visions, says, "The public majority disapproves of Christian Scientist and Jehovah's Witness parents who deny medicine to children afflicted with life-threatening illness. The public regards the anti-science attitudes of these faiths as unacceptable. Likewise, we should similarly disapprove of the withholding of any medicine or life extension practices that deter death for individuals, of any age."

Regrettably, in 2014, America continues to be permeated with an anti-life extension culture. Genetic engineering experiments in humans often have to pass numerous red-tape-laden government regulatory bodies in order to conduct any tests at all, especially at publicly funded universities and research centers. Additionally, many states still ban human reproductive cloning, which could one day play a critical part in extending human life. The current US administration is also culpable. The White House is simply not doing enough to extend American lifespans. The US Government spends just 2% of the national budget on science and medical research, while their defense budget is over 20%, according to a 2011 US Office of Management Budget chart. Do Presidents not care about this fact, or are they unaware that not actively funding and supporting life extension research indeed shortens lives?

In my philosophical novel *The Transhumanist Wager*, there is a scene which takes place outside of a California courthouse where transhumanist activists are holding up a banner. The words inscribed on the banner sum up key data:

By not actively funding life extension research, the amount of life hours the United States Government is stealing from its citizens is thousands of times more than all the American life hours lost in the Twin Towers tragedy, the AIDS epidemic, and the Vietnam War combined. Demand that your government federally fund transhuman research, nullify anti-science laws, and promote a life extension culture. The average human body can be made to live healthily and productively beyond age 150.

Some longevity experts think that with a small amount of funding—$100 billion dollars—targeted specifically towards life extension research and ending human mortality, average human lifespans could be increased by 25-50 years in about a decade's time. The world's net worth is over $200 trillion dollars, so the species can easily spare a fraction of its wealth to gain some of the most valuable commodities humans have: health and time.

Unfortunately, our species has already lost a massive amount of life hours; billions of lives have been unnecessarily cut short in the last 50 years because of widespread anti-science attitudes and policies. Even in the modern 21st Century, our evolutionary development continues to be significantly hampered by world leaders and governments who believe in non-empirical, faith-driven religious doctrines—most of which require the worship of deities whose teachings totally negate the need for radical life extension science. Virtually every major leader on the planet believes their "God" will give them an afterlife in a heavenly paradise, so living longer on planet Earth is just not that important.

Back in the real world, 150,000 people died yesterday. Another 150,000 will cease to exist today, and the same amount will disappear tomorrow. A good way to reverse this widespread deathist attitude should start with investigative government and non-government commissions examining whether public fiduciary duty requires acting in the best interest of people's health and longevity. Furthermore, investigative commissions should be set up to examine whether former and current top politicians and religious leaders are guilty of shortening people's lives for their own selfish beliefs and ideologies. Organizations and other global leaders that have done the same should be scrutinized and investigated too. And if fault or crimes against humanity are found, justice should be administered. After all, it's possible that the Catholic Church's stance on condoms will be responsible for more deaths in Africa than the Holocaust was responsible for in Europe. Over one million AIDS victims died in Africa last year alone. Catholicism is growing quickly in Africa, and there will soon be nearly 200 million Catholics on the continent.

As a civilization of advanced beings who desire to live longer, better, and more successfully, it is our responsibility to put government, religious institutions, big business, and other entities that endorse pro-death policies on notice. Society should stand ready to prosecute anyone that deliberately promotes agendas and actions that prematurely end people's useful lives. Stifling or hindering life extension science, education, and practices needs to be recognized as a legitimate crime.

****

44) A Strong-handed Government and a Basic Income Could End the Homelessness Problem in America

To visit San Francisco City Hall—a sprawling 1915 landmark that houses some of the city's most important government offices—tourists have to be careful of stepping on the homeless. The problem has become so acute, visitors are reluctant to walk around the neighborhood with young kids. Scattered on the streets and sidewalks are used hypodermic needles, garbage, and human feces

Unfortunately, the homeless problem is only getting worse, especially in big cities in California. Endless proposals from the political right and left have been suggested to deal with the Sunshine state's estimated 200,000 street people. But with exorbitant real estate prices and a dire statewide housing shortage, none work without dramatically raising taxes or ordering draconian measures.

One new proposal is different than the others. It's called a Federal Land Dividend. It wants to lease out to big business the vast federal lands America holds, and pay proceeds from this to every American adult in the form of a basic income. Estimates vary, but America owns approximately $150 trillion dollars of land and resources, much which is barely used commercially. If you divide $150 trillion dollars by 325 million American citizens, you get nearly $500,000 per person.

This half million dollar net worth is dramatically more than what the median of American individuals actually have—which is about $45,000. If we could just monetize that federal land by leasing it out at a standard 5 percent interest, we'd be able to use the income to give every adult American approximately $1700 a month indefinitely—literally ending nation-wide poverty and people's inability to afford housing. And this $1700 a month number does not include touching any US national parks whatsoever.

The key to solving the homeless situation in America is attaching a certain rider to receiving the Federal Land Dividend. If you accept this free money, you agree not to live on the streets. Should you do so, you'll forfeit your dividend—and it'll be spent on housing for you somewhere, like it or not.

While it's true that some street people have mental disease, are drug addicts, and have other issues, they're broadly functional enough to take free money and use it—especially with the myriad homeless nonprofits and services out there helping them. If homeless violate their agreement and end up back on the streets (let's say after three police warnings), they go to a homeless shelter if available (and their monthly money is given to that shelter), or they are taken to permanent housing which is paid for them from their Federal Land Dividend. There are millions of more empty rentals than homeless people in America.

Critics will say it's immoral to force street people into shelters or paid-for housing. But this would only be because they violated their binding Federal Land Dividend agreement they accepted in the first place. Besides, homeless would also have the ability to leave where they were put anytime---though why would they now that they have a real home and permanent infrastructure?

For some people, like myself, the more important part is the public's rights—not the homeless who are causing the nuisance in the first place. What about the public's right to walk on clean, cleared sidewalks in major cities where the homeless have taken over with tents and shopping carts?

A report came out recently from NBC Bay Area Investigative Unit saying San Francisco's streets were comparable to slums, and its homeless were helping to breed dangerous diseases in the public. Tax payers spend approximately $30 million dollars a year in San Francisco to clean up street people's needles and human excrement.

Additionally, transients—and the crime they commit and which are committed against them—ultimately demand extra tax payer resources from police, the fire department, and community medical services. Safety should be a right both for them and the public.

Finally, homeless women are often sexually assaulted or entrapped. Getting them off the streets could lessen domestic abuse, rape, and taking on unwanted partners in an effort to find shelter and survive.

The Federal Land Dividend can solve these issues by providing everyone enough money to find a suitable place to live. There are lots of counties in America where $1700 a month is plenty to live on, especially if combined with partners, spouses, or roommates. It might not be in San Francisco or Los Angeles, but it's not that far away either. Many places in California, like Fresno, have one and two bedroom apartments for rent for under $1000 a month.

A major benefit about the Federal Land Dividend is its bipartisan nature. The left likes it because it helps the poor and homeless. The right likes it because it grows big business without raising taxes. All that is needed to improve the lives of millions of very poor Americans is to utilize the resources and federal lands our vast nation possesses, and a little political backbone to make sure homeless use their money for housing.

****

45) Some People are Asking: Should it be Illegal to Indoctrinate Kids with Religion?

Religious child soldiers carrying AK-47s. Bullying anti-gay Jesus kids. Infant genital mutilation. Teenage suicide bombers. Child Hindu brides. No matter where you look, if adults are participating in dogmatic religions, then they are also pushing those same ideologies onto their kids.

Regardless what you think and believe, science shows human beings know very little. Our eyes register only 1 percent of the electromagnetic spectrum in the universe. Our ears detect less than 1 percent of its sound wave frequencies. Human senses—our brain's vehicles to understanding the world—leave much to be desired. In fact, our genome is only 1 percent different than that of a chimpanzee. Amazingly, despite the obvious fact no one really knows that much about what is going on with ourselves and the universe, we still insist on the accuracy of grand spiritual claims handed down to us from our barefoot forefathers. We celebrate holidays over these ancient religious tales; we choose life partners and friends over these fables; we go to war to defend these myths.

A child's mind is terribly susceptible to what it hears and sees from parents, family, and social surroundings. When the human being is born, its brain remains in a delicate developmental phase until far later in life.

"Kids are impressionable," said Dr. Eunice Pearson-Hefty, director of the Teaching Environmental Science program of Texas' Natural Resource Conservation Commission. "Anything you tell them when they're real small can have a lasting impression."

It's only later, when kids hit their teens that they begin to think for themselves and see the bigger picture. It's only then they begin to ask whether their parent's teachings make sense and are correct. However, depending on the power of the indoctrination in their childhood, people's ability to successfully question anything is likely stifled their entire lives.

In my philosophical and atheist-minded novel *The Transhumanist Wager*, protagonist Jethro Knights ends up with the ability to rewrite the social laws of the world. One important issue he faces is whether to make religion illegal altogether. There are many arguments for why religion has not been beneficial to the human race, especially in the last few centuries. In the end, a love of basic liberties prevails over Mr. Knights and he allows religion to exist. Although, he restricts religion from the public sphere, restricts religion from being integrated with education, and restricts religion from being pushed on minors.

Not surprisingly, some in the atheist and transhumanist communities feel the same way Mr. Knights does. While they may think that believing in a warmongering prophet, or a four-armed blue deity, or a spiteful God who drowns nearly all of his people is wrong, atheists and transhumanists are willing to allow it. So long as it doesn't meaningfully interfere with the world.

The problem is that it does meaningfully interfere with the world. 911 was a religious-inspired event. So was the evil of the Catholic Inquisition. And so is the quintessential conflict between Palestine and Israel. If you take "God" and "religion" out of all these happenings, you would likely find that they would not have happened at all. Instead, what you'd probably find is peaceful people and communities dedicated to preserving and improving life through reason, science, and technology—which is the essence of transhumanism and the outcome of evolution.

"Religion should remain a private endeavor for adults," says Giovanni Santostasi, PhD, who is a neuroscientist at Northwestern University Feinberg School of Medicine and runs the 20,000 person strong Facebook group Scientific Transhumanism. "An appropriate analogy of religion is that's it's kind of like porn—which means it's not something one would expose a child to."

Unfortunately, even though atheists, nonreligious people, and transhumanists number almost a billion people, it's too problematic and unreasonable to imagine taking "God" and "religion" out of the world entirely. But we do owe it to the children of the planet to let them grow up free from the ambush of belief systems that have a history of leading to great violence, obsessively neurotic guilt, and the oppression of virtually every social group that exists.

Like some other secularists and academics, I join in calling for regulation that restricts harmful religious indoctrination of children until they reach, let's say, 16 years of age. Once a kid hits their mid-teens, let them have at it—if religion is something that interests them. 16-year-olds are enthusiastic, curious, and able to rationally start exploring their world, with or without the guidance of parents. But before that, they are too impressionable to repeatedly be subjected to ideas that are faith-based, unproven, and historically wrought with danger. Forcing religion onto minors is essentially a form of child abuse, which scars their ability to reason and also limits their ability to consider the world in an unbiased manner. A reasonable society should not have to indoctrinate its children; its children should discover and choose religious paths for themselves when they become adults, if they are to choose one at all.

****

46) How Soon is Too Soon for Robot Voting Rights?

I was recently invited to be on a BBC World Service radio panel to discuss my US Presidency and third parties confronting America's two-party system. Given that public luminaries like Harvard professor Lawrence Lessig and Green Party Presidential candidate Jill Stein were also part of the 1-hour show, I resisted talking about some of my more speculative transhumanist ideas in order to focus on more pressing and current election concerns.

However, I diverged on the final question of the broadcast: *Would there be much change for third-parties in the next 10 years of US politics?* Sadly, nearly everyone said: likely not. I, however, disagreed. I believe change will come not from systematic undoing of the America's two-party monopoly, but from technology. More specifically, it will come from the plethora of thinking robots that not only may be smarter than us in 10 years, but also may require various personhood rights. That, of course, will likely mean voting rights, something I addressed when I delivered my *Transhumanist Bill of Rights* to the US Capitol last year and have also spoken about while consulting for the US Navy.

The average IQ of the human being is 100. Based on results from the Turing Test—where computers try to pretend they're human in conversation with unsuspecting users—some robots may already have nearly the equivalent IQ of adolescent humans. Generally, technology exponentially advances in sophistication, and it's not impossible that within 10 years' time the first machines will become as intelligent as the average human being.

The idea that your cell phone might soon be smarter than you is still bat-crazy to most people. But the promise of quantum computing—like the internet or CRISPR gene editing tech—could within a few years change the entire outlook of technology and how fast the field is evolving.

Ben Geortzel, an AI scientist told me that we'll likely have intelligences as smart as humans by 2029, but that they could much quicker if more money ends up in the hands of scientists. How fast we create thinking robots is likely a matter of resources, and not so much our inability to do so.

I welcome a class of thinking robots to Planet Earth, though I don't think I want any smarter than me. Despite that, they're likely to be far smarter than us, and our society as a whole will have to be aware of a new civil rights era because of them. They won't use the toilet, but they might use the outlet in the bathroom to recharge. They can always stand on public transport. Do we cut in front of them in the bank teller line?

The questions are endless. Of course, from a political point of view, they have major ramifications. There are, after all, about at least a few billion smartphones and computer devices on Earth, and even if just 10% of them figure out how to tie into the cloud and have personalities that deserve personhood, the population of voters could triple.

In America, there's much concern about voting districts, swing states, and how the Electoral College determines the Presidential election. If a robot's main server that is uses for its conscious is in Nevada, but its body is in Ohio, where does its voting right count toward the election? And if we included super smart robots to vote, does their vote count the same as humans?

I don't have all the answers to these thorny questions—some of which may need be answered by 2024. What I do know is technological growth is dramatically accelerating. And any new technology that might be born in the next half-decade could double or triple that speed. We might soon be entering a political age where robot rights and robot voting significantly alter our political process and how we elect our leaders. We better start answering those questions.

****

CHAPTER VI: TOWARD A BIGGER PICTURE

47) Do We Really Hate Trump and Clinton So Much?

I keep reading reports that say Donald Trump and Hillary Clinton are some of the most hated presidential candidates in memory. A recent NBC News/Monkey Survey poll reported six out 10 Americans dislike or even hate both of them. It's easy to confirm this feeling outside of media, too. Just look around. People everywhere— including a few billion people abroad—seem disgusted with the 2016 US elections.

However, I don't think people dislike Trump or Clinton any more than Mitt Romney or Barack Obama in 2012, or John McCain or any of the candidates before him. I think something more sinister is occurring. And I worry for 2020 and the future beyond that.

I believe a sneaky evil has grabbed hold of tens of millions of American minds and attitudes. People might all deny it, but it's happening anyway.

What is it?

Increased usage of social media and the internet has made us a nation of trolls. And there's no other good way to say it, but: Trolls are assholes.

The amount of growth Facebook has experienced in active users from 2012 to 2016 is staggering. An extra 650 million members joined worldwide in that election cycle. In the same years, Twitter— the ultimate blow-your-top-outlet-without-thinking—has grown from 340 million tweets a day to over 500 million (or 200 billion a year). In fact, many politicians and similar public personalities weren't even on Twitter in 2012. Snapchat didn't even exist until September of 2011.

One of the things that worries me most over this phenomenon is that capitalism allows us make to money off trolling. Lots of money. Like the unsavory consequences of cigarettes, Facebook wants you to get in endless heated discussions with people you don't personally know and fight it out online. Every time you click and comment, their purse grows from ad sales.

Apart from the negativity of arguing with people endlessly, I'm constantly astonished by the things people say to me on social media—knowing well that I often read them. It's not the death threats I worry about from the psychos or mentally deranged—it's the normal people that scare me. Many have good jobs, college educations, and nice families, but they still say hair-raising stuff. And it's the fact they espouse this vitriol regularly. Here's a few I got recently about me:

1) *"This guy is a fool. If you copy your mind to a machine, you are not living indefinitely, you are making a copy of yourself that may or may not life indefinitely."*

2) *"Another moron...Too much tech makes you insane in the brain."*

3) *"Satan anyone?"*

Consider the facts. I'm 6'1, 200 pounds, and I work out every day. Very few people would ever say those things to me in person, because they don't know if I'm the type to smash their teeth in (I'm not, but millions of other large males might be).

The fact is we increasingly say things online that we never would say out loud—even if it's ostensibly against our evolutionary interest. Besides being highly uncivil, this shows deep unreasonableness to me. The internet has turned us into belligerent critics. It's a direct result of the narcissism social media breeds, and it's making us into haters of most everything.

As a philosophy major in college, I studied Postmodernism, whose pop theory says humans have deconstructed existence so much that what we're intellectually left with is abject skepticism. I actually agree with this a lot, and as a result I'm quite the existentialist. But this phenomenon of American trolling is going way beyond Postmodernism and what Sartre calls nausea. It's crossing over to a feeling of loathing.

This feeling abounds in the comments sections of sites like *The Huffington Post, Breitbart,* or *Yahoo! News*—each of which can get tens of thousands of comments a day. It's common for online users on these sites to read the story title first, then the comment sections, and maybe the article (if the comments warrant it). This worrisome trend is another symptom of our times.

Reddit is maybe the ultimate trolling site, where fighting it out with comments often seems the main purpose of the site—and few people read beyond the headlines. Reddit has gained a reputation as a troll haven where young people using aliases say most anything they want. I actually like Reddit for what it is, and I think it serves its purpose. But when I see its comment quality being carried over the discussion sections of *The New York Times*, I get distressed.

Some sites are through with comments, altogether. *Vice*, where I'm an occasional columnist—recently eliminated its comments section entirely. Other media is doing this, too. One reason sites are getting rid of discussion sections is the manpower required to monitor it. Employees and editors have to delete all the unacceptable comments (many of them racist, misogynous, and even potentially illegal if they're violent threats). This costs a lot of time and money for the publication.

When I was a child and feeling upset, my mom used to make me wait 10 seconds before I said something. It was tough. I used to want to blurt out things, and immediately express my emotions. But in those 10 seconds, a lot of transformation can take place. A lot of processing and reason can emerge. My mom was right to teach me to wait. I learned to be patient, and really say what I mean, and mean what I say.

Trolling isn't a disease, it's a symptom. We can stop it by disciplining ourselves to be more civil and by respecting the inherent psychological challenges of social media use. However, if social media and comment sections of websites keep growing more raucous—and they continue to be used by more and more people— we can expect a general hate in the world to increase, until we feel loathing at most everything.

48) Wild Transhumanist Campaign Tech We'll See in the Future

I recently had the opportunity to sit down with friend and 2016 Libertarian presidential nominee Gary Johnson, who last month polled at 10 percent in general election picks. One of the things we spoke about was the future of political campaigning. Johnson won his New Mexico governorship in 1994 before the internet was being used much. Now, mastery of the internet and courting new media is a requirement to win any major election.

But the near future will be even more complex, with virtual reality, wearable tech, and holographic imagery all part of the show. The entire way a candidate runs for the presidency—from crowded rallies to handshakes at New Hampshire diners to their campaign buses—may soon change.

Politicians like Bernie Sanders already get it. He recently did a campaign event in virtual reality, a speech some are calling a historic first. Some of the advantages of campaigning in virtual reality might not be obvious. But on the YouTube video, one commentator talked about being able to get up close to read what was on Bernie's notes. That sounds cool, indeed—and not something you can't do in standard reality unless you can get past muscular security guards.

As a presidential candidate myself, I also recently gave a virtual speech in Second life. At the Terasem Annual Colloquium on the Law of Futurist Persons, I spoke to an audience that consisted of about 50 avatars—some who appeared as creatures, cyborgs, and significantly mutated transhuman beings. My own avatar—kindly created by transhuman spiritual organization Terasem for this event—looked quite like me, and even had the afternoon shadow, which apparently I'm often guilty of having.

Many experts cite President Obama's tech savvy 2008 and 2012 campaigns against John McCain and Mitt Romney, respectively, as a large reason he won. Obama was one of the first candidates to place ads in video games and other online environments. Some of his most remembered game ads were in NFL Madden 13 and NBA Live 09.

So far, no visible political candidates have really upped the ante with wearable tech, partially because we're so brainwashed with them wearing the same boring clothes for the last half century: tie, slacks, and coat. That's not to say American politics haven't been male-dominated over the last half century, or that US presidential elections, specifically, haven't always been male-dominated. Of course they have been.

But I hope that will change in the future. Built-in tech and LED lighting to candidate's shirts might enable viewers to see them better in various environments, like when it's shady outside or at night. In fact, we might be able to even feel our candidate's presence by shirts that create energy fields—or what some might call auras. At the very least, shirts could tell people candidate's moods if we wanted—already pets have collars that do that.

For me, wearable tech would be personal. In one of the biggest speeches so far of my campaign, I opened the *Financial Times* Camp Alphaville event in Europe. It was one of the hottest July London days on record at 95 degrees. Like everyone, I sweat right through my shirt—and it didn't look pleasant. I would've appreciated a shirt that could've automatically cooled me. I learned later that such innovations are on their way or already here.

But it's not just wearable tech. It's also implants. I have a small microchip in my hand—an RFID NFC implant—that can transfer business cards to smart phones with a quick hand swipe—and it's also programmed to text people: Win in 2016! It's a fun way to connect with supporters.

Coming in the future too will be augmented reality that mixes with the normal world. If Donald Trump wants a wall across the border, he can show it to us in live stream. The same can go for presidential candidate Jill Stein of the Green Party—show me 3D pie charts of how democratic socialist policies will not dramatically raise people's taxes. These tech advantages can surely help get important messages across.

Likely, the biggest change we'll see in the 2024 presidential elections (and we'll already see some in 2020) will be the use of holographic images of candidates. Already we have robots that can be Skyped through and wander around interacting with people, but the holographic image will be the real deal. Slain rapper Tupac has done some concerts this way, and it's been a big hit with fans. The holographic tech, which is already here but is currently prohibitively expensive, will likely eventually replace video conference calls.

In fact, by 2024, we're likely to have driverless campaign buses filled with only holographic images traveling in them, ready to campaign and interact with journalists. Just in case you haven't had enough of some politicians, you could have ten buses with their holograms self campaigning in all the Super Tuesday states at once.

On my campaign bus in 2016, we had drones. They were never sophisticated enough to carry things very well, but in 2020 I'm sure candidates will be using them to drop bumper stickers, carry banners at rallies, and project holographic images—including maybe fake cheering crowds.

Lest we think future elections are all about the candidates, perhaps the largest possibility on the horizon could come from digital direct democracy—the concept where citizens participate in real time input in the government. I gently advocate for a fourth branch of government, in which the people can vote on issues that matter to them and their decrees could have real legal consequence on Congress, the Supreme Court, and the Presidency.

Of course, that's only if government even exists anymore. It's possible the coming age of artificial intelligence and robots may replace the need for politicians. At least human ones. Some experts think superintelligent AI might be here in 10 to 15 years, so why not have a robot president that is totally altruistic and not susceptible to lobbyists and personal desires? This machine leader would simply always calculate the greatest good for the greatest amount of people, and go with that. No more Republicans, Democrats, Libertarians, Greens, or whatever else we are.

It's a brave new future we face, but technology will make our lives easier, more democratic, and more interesting. Additionally, it will change the game show we go through every four years called the

US Presidential elections. In fact, if we're lucky—given how crazy the 2016 elections have made America look—maybe technology will make future elections disappear altogether.

****

49) The Future of the LGBT Movement may Involve Transhumanism

The other night my wife and I were reading to our 4-year-old daughter a children's book that we borrowed from the public library. We came to a section where two characters — both who were the same sex — began having romantic feelings for each other. My wife and I smiled — we have many good LGBT friends.

Later that evening after putting my daughter to bed, I began wondering about the future of the LGBT movement, especially after Tim Cook, Apple's CEO and probably the world's most influential technologist, recently said he was proud to be gay. It's certainly interesting to speculate on how sexuality, sexual orientation, and society's interpretation of it all will change over the next 25 years as we charge headlong into the transhumanist age.

It shouldn't come as a surprise to anyone that the LGBT movement and transhumanism have a lot in common. Nearly all transhumanists support the LGBT cause. After all, a desire to be free to alter, express, and control one's sexual preference and identity sounds like a transhumanist concept. Advocates of transhumanism aim to alter, express, and control their bodies and preferences too, except they emphasize doing it with science and technology. If you look closely, the two movements — especially some of their major philosophies — are practically different sides of the same coin, and each is poised to gain strength from one another in the future as radical technologies transform the species.

In the next 25 years, the human being will undergo a larger transformation of its evolutionary body than it has undergone in the last 100,000 years. Artificial hearts will likely become better than real hearts. Telepathy via brain implants will become an important form of communication. Men will be able to give birth with implanted uteri. Each of these technologies already exists in some form and will soon be more widely available.

The million dollar question regarding these technologies is whether we will be allowed to freely use them. After all, the United States Congress is basically made up of all religious politicians, some whose faiths derive from texts that forbid anything like LGBT practices or transhumanism. Transhumanist's main goals are to overcome mortality and become as free and powerful as possible using technology—in essence, to become godlike.

For ages now, society has largely been afraid of transformation, especially when it concerns the human body or sexuality. Even today, a dozen U.S. states still have anti-sodomy laws, and LGBT people are often killed in places around the world — sometimes stoned to death — for their actions and beliefs. While victories have been won in the 21st century, such as in California and other states where people of the same sex can now officially marry, massive inequalities and bigotry still exist.

In the future, transhumanist technology and science will compliment the LGBT movement and help push it forward in the face of continued social oppression and closed-mindedness. This is important, since LGBT people are devoted to freedom. They want to be free to do anything they please without condemnation so long as it doesn't hurt others. Transhumanists — a notable number who are LGBT themselves — want the same exact thing. And they can work together to better achieve their goals.

With the onslaught of new tech and advanced medical and surgical techniques hitting the market, it's likely the LGBT movement will involve more transhumanist issues in the future. For those who are conservative and resist change, this may prove challenging. Take cybersex and virtual reality, for example, where Facebook's Oculus Rift and haptic suits will allow people from all corners of the world to have group sex if they want. Or what about fembots and sexbots, which already represent a growing 100 million dollar market? In 10 years, some robots may be as sophisticated as humans. Do we give them rights? Can we marry them? What if they're gay? What if we program them to not know if they're gay or not?

"The world is shifting under our feet," says B.J. Murphy, a pansexual transhumanist, writer, and futurist. "In 15 years, conservatives and anti-gay people will look back at the LGBT movement and yearn for an adversary so simple in its demands."

B.J. Murphy is right. The future will be anything but simple. Already, within two decade's time, parents may choose to have designer babies without certain sexual organs. Is a uterus necessary if you have ectogenesis (use of artificial wombs)? Or does it just present extra cancer risk and, for some, decades of painful, crampy menstrual cycles? Alternatively, will some religions encourage some males to be born with genetically lowered sex drives so they may have a better chance at becoming celibate priests, a shrinking vocation in the U.S.? Finally, will some seemingly narcissistic people procreate only through cloning techniques? The bizarre questions of the transhumanist age seem endless — and they are already being asked by a growing number of people.

Frankly, I could see many humans in the future stopping physical sex altogether as cranial implant technology finds precisely the right means to stimulate erogenous zones in the brain — something researchers are already working on. Real sex will probably not be able to match direct and scientifically targeted stimulation of our minds. Such actions may lead to a society where male and female traits disappear as pleasure becomes "on-demand," and gene therapy is able to combine the most functional parts of both genders into one entity. Not surprisingly, some institutions like marriage may end up going the way of the dinosaurs.

The LGBT movement has found firm footing in the 21st century — a testament to the courage of its supporters. I applaud them and support their courageous efforts. As a transhumanist, agnostic, and a political candidate, I stand ready to defend their freedoms and help their agenda forward, all the while knowing that the future will bring its own set of new challenges that none of us can easily foresee. In fact, the clash of civil rights in the transhumanist era may just be starting in a whole new way. Personhood, sexual freedom (virtual or not), and gender identity (or non-identity) will soon take on unprecedented roles in society, spurred by radical innovation and changing stereotypes of what it means to be a human being. For me, the wildcard of the future is not in society, but in the transformative technology that we invent and embrace.

50) The Age of Transhumanism Needs the European Union to Succeed

Scientific innovation doesn't just happen on its own. It takes stable economies, free societies, and open-minded governments. The best environment for science to thrive in is that of collaborating groups incentivized to communicate and cooperate with one another. This is precisely what the European Union is.

And now, more than ever, the union of Europe is needed — because we are crossing over into the transhumanist age, where radical science and technology will engulf our lives and challenge our institutions. Robots will take 75 percent of the jobs in the next 25 years. CRISPR gene editing technology will allow us to augment our intelligence, perhaps doubling our IQ. Bionic organs will stave off death, allowing 200 year lifespans.

The science and technology coming in just the next two decades will cause unprecedented challenges to humanity. Most of the world will get chip implants — I have one — to assist with quick payments, emergency tracking, and to replace archaic accessories like car keys. We'll also all use genetic therapies to cure cancer, heart disease, Alzheimer's, and even aging. And robots will be ubiquitous — driving us everywhere, homeschooling our children, and maybe even becoming preferred sexual partners.

All this change will require immense cooperation between cultures, religious, ethnicities, and nations — because the ethics of the future are more complex than the ethics of the past. Do we allow one country like America to control the first Artificial Intelligence (knowing the first act of this AI will be to make it so no other greater AI can ever be created)? Is a violent crime in virtual reality legally punishable if no one is physically harmed in the real world? Should individuals be allowed personal armed drone armies that follow them around in public?

As an American citizen, as well as a Hungarian passport holder, I feel I belong to both America and the European Union. And I know the future will be overwhelmingly complex and difficult to navigate. The best way to forge our way through the transhumanist age is as a joined union, where decisions are democratically decided to implement the greatest good for the greatest amount of people.

I write these words as a man who believes that one day America, the EU, and other nations around the world will likely unite under one democratic elected world government — making the EU an all-important test of the future. Technology will induce this geo-political change. Technology will eradicate people's differences and bring us all closer to one another. Technology will change the need for multiple languages, for multiple cultures, for multiple currencies, for multiple legal systems — even for multiple personal meanings. The facts are obvious to those who work in science and technology: Humans are evolving into cyborgs. And one day soon we will all evolve into machines and be permanently interconnected through data and code. It's the fate of evolution and progress.

For these reasons, I believe the UK should stay in the EU. Too much is at stake with the coming age of radical science and transhumanism to change the most unified political structure the world knows. Collaboration, cooperation, and increased globalization are what we need now — and a lot of luck for the future.

****

51) Will Capitalism Survive the Coming Robot Revolution?

Economic experts are trying to figure out a question that just two decades ago seemed ridiculous: If 90 percent of human jobs are replaced by robots in the next 40 years — something now considered plausible — is capitalism still the ideal economic system to champion? No one is certain about the answer, but the question is making everyone nervous — and forcing people to dig deep inside themselves to discover the kind of future they want.

After America beat Russia in the Cold War, most of the world generally considered capitalism to be the hands-down best system on which to base economies and democracies. For decades, few doubted capitalism's merit, which was made stronger by thriving globalization and a skyrocketing world net worth. In 1989 — when the Berlin Wall fell — the world had only 198 billionaires. Now, according to Forbes, there are 1,826 of them in 2016.

Despite growing riches, when banks collapsed in 2007 during the Great Recession, the world stepped back and wondered aloud if a more nuanced approach to economic progress was needed. These doubts of 21st century capitalism helped set the stage for an economic paradigm shift just starting to appear — economists observing jobs not just disappearing to other countries, but disappearing off the face of the Earth. The culprit: robots and software.

At first, the warnings of this weren't very loud. After all, economies and companies thrive because of modernization, which includes upgrading with new tech to make and save money. But in the last year, a growing chorus of people are beginning to see a tipping point, maybe a decade in the future, where tens of millions of jobs may be lost in as short as a five-year period — which would be many more times the jobs lost during the Great Recession.

Already today, there are countries trying out driverless trucks to deliver goods. Truck driving is one of the most prevalent jobs in America, with about 3.5 million drivers. What will we do in five years if they are replaced with vehicles that don't need human intervention to get on and off a highway to deliver goods?

Of course, they are just one occupation amongst many dozens — like waiters, bank tellers and even librarians — that might no longer require humans in the very near future.

Capitalism says this is the nature of the competitive economy. However, those jobs that are replaced will never be regained, and truck drivers and waiters will not easily find other jobs. Many will likely need to be provided for by the state, otherwise grown men and women will surely pick up Molotov cocktails and show the world a thing or two about worker revolutions.

The only difference between this and other historical revolutions is they won't be alone. This time it's not a problem of the rich versus the poor. In 20 years, everyone's job will be at stake, even that of my wife, who trained 19 years in college to become a practicing Ob/Gyn — and still today has $100,000+ in school debt. But machines will deliver babies and remove cervical cancer better than people. And software will do taxes more efficiently than accountants. And articles will be crafted better by news aggregating software than living, breathing journalists.

Everyone, including even the U.S. president, is at risk of being outperformed by a machine — and eventually being jobless and without income.

So, now that we know we're all going to lose our jobs, what system can make it so humans will still be happy and live better without employment? Clearly, it's not capitalism.

Whichever system we choose will have to incorporate an improving standard of life for people and society. For this reason, I tend to support a Universal Basic Income as one way to desire robots to take our jobs but not leave the world poor. However, that doesn't really say what will happen to economies after the robot revolution is really underway.

Some people have said a fully automated luxury communism will prevail once robots take all the jobs — an economic system that favors technology pampering humans all day long. Communism is a historically loaded word that few people like (including myself, a longtime entrepreneur).

Additionally, it insinuates being chained to community and social service, something I think our individualistic-minded world may scoff at. The 21st century has made people feel more entitled than ever, and, frankly, with so much amazing innovation humans have come up with, we deserve it. We deserve to be pampered by technology. We deserve to never again work a day in our lives if we don't want to. We deserve not to be bothered by government or society if we're not bothering others. And we deserve to pursue lofty dreams instead struggling to earn a handful of dollars.

In fact, I doubt money will even survive this century. If anything, in the future, only knowledge will have tradable value — the knowledge to create better machines, software and experiences from technology. Around this time — surely before 2075 — the singularity will be possible, a point where people connect themselves to artificial intelligence and essentially disappear into a sea of growing and organizing information. Then it's anyone's guess what happens to the world.

However, back to reality here in 2016: Whatever economic system does prevail in the next 25 years, it won't be like anything we thought of before. Karl Marx and Adam Smith simply did not account for what indefinite robot labor would mean to a new world increasingly reliant on microprocessors and 1s and 0s for its every step forward.

Whatever happens, it's probably best to keep an open mind about the future and new economic models. Many of us are running on a financial treadmill right now, trying to get ahead and realize the American Dream of riches and the good life. But in the future, the American Dream may be more about discovery of our newly acquired transhuman possibilities and enjoying the technology that has made our modern lives so simple and easy. I think I can get used to that.

****

52) The #MeToo Movement has Backfired— Females Everywhere are Being Punished

Everywhere I go, male friends of mine are newly on alert. Whether they're CEOs in my hometown of San Francisco, candidates running political campaigns, or journalists writing articles, men are increasingly wary of women. They're scared to hire them as often; they're not going out to dinner with them as often; as journalists they're not even reporting about them as frequently, for fear of getting themselves inadvertently in trouble. The MeToo movement has put many men on extreme guard, and the simplest way for men to preserve their careers and persona in the age of "shoot first, look later" social media is simply to avoid women.

The net result is that women are getting bypassed professionally, intellectually, and emotionally in ways that resemble the 1950s—undoing generations of hard work by women who rightfully wanted and deserved equality with men.

How did we get here? The MeToo movement originally aimed to highlight sexual abuse and harassment. Approximately 2-3 million Americans—mostly women and children—are assaulted in some way every year in the US. It's a tragic epidemic.

But in an increasing number of high-profile cases, the MeToo movement has moved from accusing male abusers with factual comprehensive evidence to casting subjective judgement based on decades' old memories about old flings via social media. Careers and reputations—as well as current relationships and marriages—are being affected and sometimes ruined in just hours.

I think if women—or anyone for that matter—are accosted, harassed, and foul play has been committed against them, it needs to be called out in one very simple way: Report it to the police immediately and try to file charges. There are very good laws, abuse tests, and detective methods to protect most anybody from anything legitimately harmful.

Otherwise, it's usually just someone's word against another. And the legal system doesn't, thankfully, make judgements based on that unless guilt is admitted.

I want to be clear: I understand that women have been unfairly mistreated for centuries, and that men have had it far easier in life in general. I also understand that sometimes, the pendulum of justice swings too far in the other direction when trying to right a wrong—and that enough time will correct all things, and maybe men should be more patient with MeToo as a whole. But this swift pendulum of MeToo has created a type of vicious and fascist cultural response—often driven by angry feminists aiming to be political weapons—that can threaten the very food both men (and their spouses) put on the table for their children. The media—sometimes from publishing companies barely surviving financially—often make it far worse too for professionals and public figures by obsessively running click-bait MeToo accusation stories of them, including sometimes those stories with no legal or journalistic merit.

Another significant factor is that the men who don't care about MeToo concerns are generally not the ones in charge of, reshaping, or moving society forward. On the other hand, beta guys are still available for anything, and women can date them freely and easily, as these guys have little to lose. The problem here is these aren't the guys many women want, and yet women are being increasingly forced to date them due to the forces at work in the MeToo movement. As a father of two young girls, this significantly bothers me, since I'd love to see my daughters grow up in a world where they have as much opportunity as possible in the dating world to find the best partner (and not have the best potential partners see my daughters as possible threats). My wife, a physician at Planned Parenthood, feels the same way I do.

The majority of alpha men don't physically abuse or consciously harass women under any circumstances. Yet all alpha men now must be perpetually on guard, and it's simply easier for them to build careers in relative isolation then worry about constantly dating and having flirtatious flings. In this way, the MeToo movement has spectacularly backfired—and its results will last years, if not decades.

To truly succeed, the MeToo movement needed to call itself: #CallPoliceImmediatelyAfterYou'veBeenMistreated. That is the movement that's needed in America to stop sexual assault and harassment.

****

53) Calling on America to Establish a Longevity Peace Prize

In early 2018 I had the opportunity to meet with Lars Heikensten, executive director of the Nobel Foundation. We were at Congreso Futuro, South America's major science conference, where I shared the aims of transhumanism. Namely, to allow people to overcome death and to live indefinitely through the use of radical science and technology.

Talking with Heikensten got me thinking about the benefits of a global-reaching public prize for longevity. The transhumanist movement currently receives little recognition outside of scientific circles; having an international award like the Nobel prizes would help it spread, to the benefit of all society.

Why shouldn't we reward efforts and discoveries in longevity with the same accolades we bestow on people who advance other scientific fields, create important bodies of literature, or fight for world peace?

Our societies already reflect an accelerating desire to stop aging. Think of the advances of knowledge, science, and perspectives we could achieve if we had more time and experience. Think of how equipped we would be to fix problems in the future, if we had already lived through the failings and discoveries of past centuries?

As it turns out, I'm not the only one pondering these questions. Earlier this year, I traveled to the Los Angeles headquarters of the XPRIZE Foundation, which awards prizes for "industry-changing technology that brings us closer to a better, safer, more sustainable world." I had been invited along with about 60 other longevity advocates to help develop a possible prize surrounding longevity. I was ecstatic.

The two-day brainstorming event, hosted by founder Peter Diamandis and opened with a keynote by inventor and futurist Ray Kurzweil, was like a historic secret gathering filled with noted longevity scientists planning on conquering death. Among other luminaires in attendance was Sergey Young, creator of the $100 million Longevity Vision Fund. During some of the heated sessions, medical doctors and anti-aging researchers argued loudly across the conference room about biomarkers, enzymes, telomerase endings of genes, and how far mitochondria might be manipulated.

Frankly, I felt a little out of my element—I'm not a scientist, but a communicator. My original proposal, designed later with the help of Max More, Natasha Vita-More, James Strole, and Bernadeane, was called the Longevity Peace Prize. It would award a one-time $5 million prize to a person or a group who convinces a government to publicly classify aging as a disease.

Radical longevity—also called life extension or anti-aging science—is in the midst of a massive shift. In the last several months, the amount of investment in various longevity-focused products and endeavors has jumped drastically, from millions to many billions of dollars.

In the past year Google upped its investment by $1.5 billion in anti-aging venture with its Calico Life Sciences. This year Bank of America analysts predicted the longevity industry could be worth "at least $600 billion" by 2025.

Gerontologist Aubrey de Grey says we are just a decade or two away from achieving "robust rejuvenation" milestones that will give us treatments to eliminate many diseases, and start to stop aging. Experiments with rodents have already had success with rejuvenating aged organs. Technologists in Silicon Valley are already taking FDA-approved drugs like metformin to make themselves live longer.

Genetic editing therapy, which can reprogram a gene to not age, is a front runner in anti-aging science. Human experiments are already underway to test the technology. Bionic organs (like artificial hearts) and stem cell therapies are also being developed by dozens of companies designing products to expand healthy lifespans.

In spite of major progress in the scientific community of longevity research—and major resources being invested in the field by leading companies and organizations—many people around the world are unaware that radical life extension research exists as a real thing. Many others are downright skeptical of it.

But the science is already here. And it will inevitably impact how we innovate and solve problems in every major field; from climate science, to politics, to education and health care systems. A major international longevity prize would help societies shift their thinking and become more aware about how deeply the field will alter our future, and how much sooner major shifts will occur than is generally acknowledged.

Historically speaking, prizes targeted at specific issues have garnered a lot of attention, and led to important advances. They also create a public discourse that garners social accountability in a field by improving visibility and allowing more people to weigh in and speak up and participate more in how funding is allocated via awards. The Field's Medal, awarded to mathematicians under 40 years old, has inspired important changes in math departments around the world. A Pulitzer Prize in journalism often forever changes not only a person's career, but the power of influence of a person's work. Even winning an Oscar at the Academy Awards has helped drive cultural trends and changes.

Few goals of humanity could so dramatically alter the lives of humans as extreme longevity. The field is ripe for a significant award. If people start living to the age of 500—which Bill Maris, former head of Google Ventures says is possible—so many current ideas about human life would change, including ones that impact us personally such as marriage, child-rearing, and retirement.

At the XPRIZE Foundation gathering of futurists earlier this year, my Longevity Peace Prize was the only one of the 16 proposals put forth that was based in longevity activism.

The other proposals targeted scientific achievements such as creating specific human longevity biomarkers, targeting dementia with innovative remediation medicine, and carrying 3D printed or stem cell grown hearts around in cryo-boxes for rushed transplants. As these were all heavily science based, they require teams of medical researchers to complete the missions. After a group vote, my award came in eighth and did not make the top-five cut, now being further reviewed by XPRIZE staff for possible award development.

I applaud my science-minded colleagues in the workshop, and I love the amazing work of the XPRIZE. But for longevity culture and awareness to spread around the world, we will need a prize that target audiences outside of the science and medical communities.

Transformative prizes go way beyond their fields; they inspire everyday people to think differently and learn something new about where the world is heading. And just like the Nobel Peace Prize, anybody should be able to win them for doing something important and beneficial for the world, like getting humans to live far longer than they currently do.

Much of the world thinks of death as natural, and that to interfere with it would be to spite nature and future generations. For most of the world's population, there's also a positive religious implication to death and the opportunity to meet one's maker.

I have spent much of my professional career trying to tell people why living dramatically longer is essential to humanity. I don't want to die ever, and I think it's tragic that individual humans are only here for 80 years or so.

It's been a long and ongoing battle for me to convince the public that people should try to live far longer. Currently, governments don't back projects or fund initiatives that consider aging controversial, much less a disease.

And yet billionaire after billionaire is starting to enter the life extension field and invest in it—everyone from Larry Ellison to Peter Theil to Mark Zuckerberg, who recently donated $3 billion dollars to wipe out all disease by the end of the century.

While this is excellent news for the longevity industry, a society that embraces living super long must have more than the one-percenters backing it. It must have the government and national culture supporting it as well. And it needs to be accessible to people no matter who they are.

A high-profile annual global prize for longevity could be just the answer to engaging more people around the world with the developments in the longevity industry. Death and aging impacts everyone, not just the super wealthy, highly-educated populations. Radical longevity should have the same reach, and be available to everyone.

If I could wave a magic wand—and stay within reasonable financial boundaries—I'd create an annual $1 million prize and award it to the person who has had the most positive impact on the public. This award could be for a scientist, a politician, a celebrity, an artist, a philosopher, or just anyone vehemently committed to anti-aging, who creates a true and felt impact in the longevity domain. Importantly, this award committee should focus on longevity pioneers outside of the direct medical or scientific fields.

My visions is for a peace price, not a medical prize, because living indefinitely is not only about aging, it's also about dealing with our biggest problems, like overpopulation, growing inequality, skyrocketing environmental concerns, and trying to improve living standards for the elderly. Extreme longevity will affect social security burdens, religious beliefs, the health care system, and families who might now regularly have multi-generations living under one roof.

An annual $1 million award would require about a $50 million dollars investment, a small nonprofit foundation to manage the award and its finances, and a good publicity team to organize media attention. There would also need to be a well-planned yearly award ceremony. A $50 million investment may seem like a lot of money, but many one-time donations to universities other non-profit organizations far surpass that.

Isn't our future, and how it is shaped, a matter that concerns all of us? If we have something like a major longevity award, people can participate in how we adapt to longevity, rather than deal with decisions made in closed meetings and medical labs. If we are to celebrate the work of those who are trying to get humans to live dramatically longer, we need to be a part of the conversation from the start.

I'm still hoping some wealthy patron, organization, university, or government might establish a yearly longevity prize that the world will cheer on. As the future comes closer, people should be aware of what longevity scientists and advocates are working on, and how the specter of death might one day be significantly diminished—whether you like it or not. We all need to be ready for that reality when it arrives.

****

54) Will Transhumanism Change Racism in the Future?

Despite decades of progress, racism and bigotry are still prevalent in the United States. Often, they even dominate the news in American media, like during the Baltimore riots or the Ferguson shooting. Movements like Black Lives Matter remind us that the society we live in still has many biases to be fought against, but that good work can be done to combat bigotry if people unite against it.

Despite this, the quest to find true equality in the world is about to get more complicated. It's possible the ability to completely change skin color may arrive in the next 10-20 years. Like a chameleon, expect humans to literally change their skin color and texture soon through coming technologies—most that will probably be based on genetic editing.

Already, humans have the technology to change the color of eyes and choose the sex of their offspring. But on the horizon are new techniques—based on CRISPR genetic editing technology—that may permanently or temporarily alter the melanin in our skin (the pigment mostly responsible for its color). And like some characters in the X-Men film series, we may even be able to do this in real-time someday.

Transhumanists with Do-It-Yourself CRISPR kits are already experimenting with the technology. But few formal scientists have dared to question how and if CRISPR may change race issues in the future.

In a conversation with *CBS News*, Dr. Arthur Caplan, founding director of the division of medical ethics at NYU Langone Medical Center's Department of Population Health, evaded the question:

CBS News asked: *Does that mean scientists will be able to engineer changes to eye or skin color, or give people mega-strength?*

"Maybe." said Caplan. "I think it's reasonable to presume you could tweak things for strength, more muscles, endurance, or to be able to run or travel further." You might be able to enhance memory, to make a person able to retain more or learn faster, he said.

"Someday," he said, "I think you could tweak genes that would allow you to perceive more. You might be able to see more like a bat, sense more of the radiation spectrum. See ultraviolet light and parts of the energy spectrum we don't see but that other creatures do. Eagle-eye vision."

"You could certainly make people more disease resistant, less likely to get a cold or the flu. Or to fight off MRSA or E. coli — build up their immune systems. Enhance them so they could enjoy more pleasure. They've been doing a teeny, tiny bit in animals," said Caplan, who will lead sessions on ethical and regulatory issues of gene editing in animal research next week in Washington, DC.

I don't blame Caplan for not answering the loaded part of the question from CBS. It's a thorny subject to think that a technology we already have in our hands can literally change the very physicality of our beings.

Of course, it's not just changing skin color that's controversial. There are transhumanists who want to grow tails, horns, and even fish gills so they can breathe underwater. And some are already trying to do it. My favorite experiment of transhumanists is the attempt to create photosynthesis capabilities in their bodies—in an effort to feed themselves for free and end world hunger by getting energy directly from the sun.

These new citizen scientist experiments go under the banner of biohacking—and it's quickly become one of the fastest growing aspects of transhumanism. Many biohackers are millennials and aiming to revolutionize what it means to be human.

Biohackers also make me think of the original *Star Wars* movie where Luke Skywalker first meets Hans Solo amongst a plethora of strange-looking creatures in a rough bar on planet Tatooine. Such a scene in real life is no longer just possible, but likely now given CRISPR technology.

I'm guessing that genetic editing techniques and bionic fabrication will allow us to do things to our bodies we never thought possible. In fact, with the growing of neuro-technology advances, there is now even talk of adding a third eye on the back of the head in biohacker communities. Some blind people have robotic eyes that already enable them to see.

If you're asking yourself if this is all ethical, the real question is: Why isn't it ethical? Transhumanists believe we should be able to do anything we want with our bodies so long as it's not hurting others, a staple of the newly written *Transhumanist Bill of Rights*.

Bear in mind ideas like this have long been underway already. For example, transgender surgery has become more common. And 3D printed body parts also are being used to help people in need. And many older persons are already a cyborg in some way or another, having artificial hips, dentures, or something else synthetic in them. I have a RFID chip in my hand that allows me to start a car without keys.

All these technologies and advances aside, the Tatooine bar in *Star Wars* highlights another aspect of future racism—that of droids versus biological creatures. In the bar, the bartender—upon seeing Luke Skywalker with C-3PO and R2-D2—shouts: "We don't serve their kind here."

Robots are just about to make their entrance into the world in a big way, occupying households, helping with chores, and teaching our kids mathematics. In fact, on my cross country presidential campaign bus tour, I traveled with a 4-foot robot onboard. Everyone loved the machine, but if they had known it was videoing everything, would they still be as enthused?

Some of these issues were brought up recently with Google Glass, where resistance was met with the technology in public. I also own this device. People always give me strange, cynical looks, especially if I wear my Google Glass into a restaurant or at a non-tech conference.

Of course, racism has one more major new arena of technology to contend with—that of the virtual world. Avatars can basically be designed to appear in any way someone wants. So people can represent themselves to others in totally different ways. Some might say the avatar is a costume, but early reports of virtual hate and rape online have shown that people (mainly their feelings but sometimes their bodies as in the case of a hacked Vibease vibrator) can indeed be hurt, and such a thing can even have legal consequence.

Through the use of new technologies, society will have to grapple with continued forms of bigotry in the everchanging landscape of being human. But skin color may soon not be the dominant theme of racism, but rather the choice of what appearance we choose to reveal ourselves. I hope the diversity that technology gives us on who to be will make us far more accepting of each other and our multitude of personalities and behaviors.

****

55) Capitalism 2.0: The Economy of the Future will be Powered by Neural Prosthetics

A battle for the "soul" of the global economy is underway. The next few decades will likely decide whether capitalism survives or is replaced with a techno-fueled quasi-socialism where robots do most of the jobs while humans live off government support, likely a designated guaranteed or basic income.

Many experts believe wide-scale automation is inevitable. Even the world's largest hedge fund, Bridgewater Associates, recently announced it's building an AI to replace its managers, many of whom are highly educated and previously thought invulnerable to automation. Robots, it seems, will manage everything. Or will they?

A next-generation technology, likely to arrive in five to 10 years, is being credited as the savior of capitalism. Known today as neural prosthetics, or neural lace, it's essentially tech that reads your brainwaves. This tech promises to connect our brains to the cloud and AI to link us with machines using thought alone.

While this technology sounds farfetched, hundreds of thousands of people globally have implants connected to their brains. Up till now, all of them have been implanted for medical reasons, with the most common being the cochlear implant which allows the deaf to hear by stimulating the auditory nerve. Increasingly, patients with

Parkinson's and Alzheimer's are testing out the technology in the hope of staving off their diseases. And President Obama's BRAIN initiative, announced in 2013, allocated $70 million to government-funded DARPA to jumpstart the field of brain implants.

For humans to beat the machines, or at least be competitive, we're going to have to follow this path; to connect with them directly.

One California startup founded by entrepreneur Bryan Johnson is called Kernel. Kernel wants to build a neural prosthetic that would allow humans, among other things, to keep up with the machines in real time, similar to a human mind literally being connected to the internet and all its algorithms and search functions.

Elsewhere, Elon Musk recently announced plans to start a neural lace company called Neuralink. Known for making wild tech bets, Musk said in Dubai, in March: "Over time I think we will probably see a closer merger of biological intelligence and digital intelligence." In particular, he hopes to have success with his new company in just five years' time.

The challenging reality suggests that if humans don't develop these implants or headsets, hundreds of millions of jobs will be lost to robots. Some, like myself, even believe Wall Street will be emptied of human traders. The same automation takeover will also likely hit law offices, engineering firms, and even politicians might one day be replaced by machines that seek only to help the people through the best, most altruistic algorithms.

Neural prosthetics will eliminate that. It will preserve competition – not only in the human race, but against machines. For those, like me, who appreciate most parts of capitalism and what it's done for progress and innovation, that's a good thing.

But it'll take more than just a mind tapped into the cloud to be widely competitive in the overall job market. Augmented limbs, bionic organs, and widespread use of exoskeleton technology will be needed to compete against robotic strength.

For years I've been supportive of a basic income, which would provide a monthly income for the poor – mostly because I saw it as the only logical way to keep people fed and housed, while still allowing for technological and economic evolution. Now, with neural prosthetics and upgraded bodies, I see the future may, instead, be full of capitalistic enterprise, fueled by transhumanist technologies that allow us to more closely resemble the machines.

That's not to say I'm abandoning my views on basic income. Instead, I believe there will be another aspect to the future economy that isn't only for the robot and AI manufacturers, but for hundreds of millions – maybe billions – of people willing to use tech to compete against machines. A future motto of humanity and capitalism might be: "If you can't beat a machine, become one." As a radical science and technology advocate, that's a philosophy I can support.

****

APPENDIX

ESSAYS

1) A version of *The Growing World of Transhumanism* first appeared in *The American Conservative*

2) A version of *We Must Transition from a Military-Industrial Complex into A Science-Industrial Complex* first appeared in *HuffPost*

3) A version of *The Only Way to Fix the Earth's Environmental Issues is via New Technology* first appeared in *Vice*

4) A version of *Technology Will Replace the Need for Big Government* first appeared in *Vice*

5) A version of *Transhumanism is Under Siege from Socialism* first appeared in *The Maven*

6) A version of *Genetic Editing Could Cause the Next Cold War* first appeared in *Vice*

7) A version of *An AI Global Arms Race is Looming* first appeared in *Vice*

8) A version of *Secular Advocate: Religion is Harming Society and Lives* first appeared in *HuffPost*

9) A version of *The New American Dream: Let the Robots Take our Jobs* first appeared in *Vice*

10) A version of *The Abortion Debate is Stuck. Artificial Wombs are the Answer* first appeared in *The New York Times*

11) A version of *In the Transhumanist Age We Should be Fixing Disabilities not Sidewalks* first appeared in *Vice*

12) A version of *I Advocate for the Legalization of All Drugs* first appeared in *Vice*

13) A version of *Let's End Incarceration and Use Tech to Supervise Criminals* first appeared in *Vice*

14) A version of *How Technology Could Facilitate and then Destroy Immigration* first appeared in *Vice*

15) A version of *Space Exploration Will Spur Transhumanism and Mitigate Existential Risk* first appeared in *TechCrunch*

16) A version of *Is it Time for a Transhumanist Olympics?* first appeared in *HuffPost*

17) A version of *How to End Taxes Forever* first appeared in *Vice*

18) A version of *Mass Shootings and Terrorism can be Stopped by Drones, Robots, and AI Scanners* first appeared in *The Daily Dot*

19) A version of a *A Federal Land Dividend Could Provide a Universal Basic Income* first appeared in *Business Insider*

20) A version of *The Transhumanist Party's Founder on the Future of Politics* first appeared in *Vice*

21) A version of *In the Age of Longer Lifespans, Should College be Mandatory?* first appeared in *Vice*

22) A version of *There is an Alternative to Lawyers Running the Country* first appeared in *Vice*

23) A version of *The Second Amendment Isn't Prepared for a 3-D Printed Army* first appeared in *Vice*

24) A version of *We Need a New Government Agency and Tort Reform to Conquer all Disease* first appeared in *Vice*

25) A version of *We Must Destroy Nukes Before an Artificial Intelligence Learns to Use Them* first appeared in *Vice*

26) A version of *How Brain Implants (and Other Technology) Could Make the Death Penalty Obsolete* first appeared in *Vice*

27) A version of *Could Direct Digital Democracy and a New Branch of Government Improve the US?* first appeared in *Vice*

28) A version of *Could an Implant Have Saved the Life of the Toddler Attacked by the Disney World Alligator?* first appeared in *The Daily Dot*

29) A version of *Reparations: I Became a Pot Felon at 18. I'm Owed More than an Apology* first appeared in *Reason*

30) *Should People Who Pay Zero Federal Income Taxes be Allowed to Vote in Federal Elections?* was first published in this book

31) A version of *Forget Trump, Zoltan Istvan Wants to be the 'Anti-Death' President* first appeared in *Wired UK*

32) A version of *Why a Presidential Candidate is Driving a Giant Coffin Called the Immortality Bus Across America* first appeared in *HuffPost*

33) A version of *Zoltan Istvan: Immortality Bus delivers Transhumanist Bill of Rights to US Capitol* first appeared in *International Business Times*

34) A version of *What I Learned Running for President and Election Changes that Should be Made* first appeared in *Vice*

35) A version of *Revolutionary Politics are Necessary for Transhumanism to Succeed* first appeared in *Vice*

36) A version of *Meet the Futurist Political Parties* first appeared in *Gizmodo*

37) A version of *Why I'm Running for California Governor as a Libertarian* first appeared in *Newsweek*

38) A version of *The Future of Libertarianism Could be Radically Different* first appeared in *The Daily Dot*

39) A version of *The Problem with the Libertarian Party* first appeared in *The Daily Caller*

40) A version of *The Privacy Enigma: Liberty Might be Better Served by Doing Away with Privacy* first appeared in *Vice*

41) A version of *A Post-Earther Perspective: Environmentalists are Wrong, Nature isn't Sacred* first appeared in *The Maven*

42) A version of *Will Licensing Parents Save Children's Lives & Improve Society?* first appeared in *Wired UK*

43) A version of *When Does Hindering Life Extension Science Become a Crime?* first appeared in *Psychology Today*

44) *A Strong-handed Government and a Basic Income Could End the Homelessness Problem in America* was first published in this book

45) A version of *Some People are Asking: Should it be Illegal to Indoctrinate Kids with Religion?* first appeared in *HuffPost*

46) A similar article of *How Soon is Too Soon for Robot Voting Rights?* first appeared in *New Scientist*

47) A version of *Do We Really Hate Trump and Clinton So Much?* first appeared in *Vice*

48) A version of *Wild Transhumanist Campaign Tech We'll See in the Future* first appeared in *Vice*

49) A version of *The Future of the LGBT Movement may Involve Transhumanism* first appeared in *HuffPost*

50) A version of *The Age of Transhumanism Needs the European Union to Succeed* first appeared in *Psychology Today*

51) A version of *Will Capitalism Survive the Coming Robot Revolution?* first appeared in *TechCrunch*

52) *The #MeToo Movement has Backfired—Females Everywhere are Being Punished* was first published in this book

53) A version of *Calling on America to Establish a Longevity Peace Prize* first appeared in *Quartz*

54) A version of *Will Transhumanism Change Racism in the Future?* first appeared in *HuffPost*

55) A version of *Capitalism 2.0: The Economy of the Future will be Powered by Neural Prosthetics* first appeared in *Wired UK*

****

AUTHOR'S BIOGRAPHY

With his popular 2016 US Presidential run as a science candidate, bestselling book *The Transhumanist Wager*, and powerful speeches at institutions like the World Bank and World Economic Forum, Zoltan Istvan has spearheaded the transformation of transhumanism into a thriving worldwide phenomenon. He is often cited as the global leader of the radical science movement. Formerly a journalist for National Geographic, Zoltan frequently writes for major media, appears on television, and also consults for organizations like the US Navy and government of Dubai. His futurist work, speeches, and promotion of radical science have reached hundreds of millions of people. A graduate of Columbia University in Philosophy and Religion, Zoltan lives in San Francisco with his physician wife and two young daughters. Visit his website at: www.zoltanistvan.com